Mary Baker Eddy In A New Light

Mary Baker Eddy

Mary Baker Eddy
In A New Light

by

Fernand E. d'Humy

Library Publishers

New York

Printed in the United States of America

"By its own volition, not a blade of grass springs up, not a spray buds within the vale, not a leaf unfolds its fair outlines, not a flower starts from its cloistered cell."

(*Science and Health*, p. 191)
MARY BAKER EDDY

CHAPTER

1

THE ANCESTRY OF MARY BAKER gave her some qualities which enabled her to transcend the accepted rules that governed the religious denominations with which her parents and friends were associated during her formative years.

The child owed to her maternal ancestry some of the qualities of courage and initiative. Her great-grandmother, Hannah Lovewell, born one hundred years earlier, was the daughter of Captain John Lovewell, who had lost his life in Pigwacket, Maine, in warfare with Indians. Captain Lovewell's father had served as an ensign in Oliver Cromwell's army. The forebears of the girl's paternal grandmother had come to America to seek religious liberty. Thus there is evident in them the same spirit of independence coupled with self-sacrifice and courage which animated their descendant.

Her mother, Abigail Ambrose of Pembroke, was the daughter of Deacon Nathaniel Ambrose, by whose name the Congregational Church in Pembroke became known. The ancestry of Mark Baker, Mary's father, can be traced to John Baker, a freeman in Charlestown, Massachusetts, in 1764. Perhaps it was in part from his forebears that Mark Baker inherited his strong character, for Mary's father was a religious man and possessed considerable administrative ability.

Her mother, Abigail, was a refined, intellectual woman who was, at the same time, quite practical in her household affairs. She exhibited a sympathetic attitude toward all. With the manifold duties associated with farm life in the early days, her time was well filled. Nevertheless she managed to take time to help the sick and needy.

Mary was born on July 16, 1821, and there were already in the family three boys, Samuel, Albert and George, and two girls, Abigail and Martha. Their grandmother was a member of the household and it was natural for her to assume charge of the new arrival so that the busy mother could attend to her many household duties. With a heart filled with love and with a special solicitation to God, the grandmother bestowed upon the child the name Mary. Her mother formalized it as Mary Morse Baker.

Thus, she entered this world with a substantial background. Her spiritual inheritance, coupled with her varied experiences and trials as she progressed through life, help to account for her accomplishments. It is recognized that mental faculties, to an extent, are inherited from ancestors.

Love was the dominant attribute which accompanied Mary into this world. Those of her ancestors who bore the family name "Lovewell" cannot be ignored in considering Mary's background. The word "love" in itself can inductively carry forward its beneficent meaning through successive generations, and most likely this family name projected definite influence for good to all those inheriting the name who left themselves open to its beneficent influence. One may surmise that the original ancestor upon whom this name was bestowed must have merited it through harboring love to a marked degree.

In Mary's genealogy it is noted that Captain John Lovewell's father served as ensign in Cromwell's army. Anyone serving as an officer under Oliver Cromwell would have been likely to come under the pious influence of the great English protector who was not only a great statesman and soldier but a man who held a profound reverence for the law of God which he carried with him into the army. He was a sworn soldier of the Decalogue. An example of his deeply rooted piety is indicated in the following quote from that admirable biography *Oliver Cromwell* by Edwin Paxton Hood:

> Sir John Goodricke used to relate a remarkable anecdote which we should probably assign to the siege of Knaresborough Castle in 1646, and which was told

him when a boy, by a very old woman, who had form-
erly attended his mother in the capacity of midwife.

"When Cromwell came to lodge in our house, in
Knaresborough," said she, "I was then but a young girl.
Having heard much talk about the man, I looked at
him in wonder. Being ordered to take a pan of coals,
and air his bed, I could not, during the operation,
forbear peeping over my shoulder several times to ob-
serve the extraordinary person, who was seated at the
far side of the room untying his garters. Having aired
the bed, I went out, and shutting the door after me,
stopped and peeped through the keyhole, when I saw
him rise from his seat, advance to the bed, and fall on
his knees, in which attitude I left him for some time.
When returning again, I found him still at prayer; and
this was his custom every night so long as he stayed at
our house."

The measure of a person's sincerity cannot be better taken
than during moments of strict privacy.

But thou, when thou prayest, enter into thy closet,
and when thou hast shut thy door, pray to thy Father
which is in secret; and thy Father which seeth in secret
shall reward thee openly. (Matthew 6:6)

The old woman's story tells how well Cromwell followed this
injunction. There was no doubt he loved God and that inherent
love in him played an important part in his affairs.

Ensign Lovewell appears to have been a good man through inheritance and was probably responsive to the spiritual qualities
of Oliver Cromwell, his commander. Thus reinforcements were
added to his own good qualities and were passed on to the
future through successive progeny, in due time reaching Mary
Baker. And so it was that the spirit of love, the love of God,
was potentially with her when she entered this world. In later
years she wrote: " 'God is Love.' More than this we cannot ask,

higher we cannot look, farther we cannot go." (*Science and Health*, p. 6.)

*

It is interesting to reason that God creates paths for the guidance and expression of His love; that great men and great women are not the product of chance; that they are appointed by God to do His work on earth. Their tasks are not always performed easily, yet the difficulties that beset their steps usually serve as schooling and preparation for the mission which is to be theirs.

These thoughts were well expressed by that great organizer of the Unitarian Movement, William Ellery Channing. In his essay "Self-Culture" he says:

> The father and mother of an unnoticed family, who, in their seclusion, awaken the mind of a child to the idea and love of perfect goodness, who awaken in him a strength of will to repel all temptation, and who send him out prepared to profit by the conflicts of life, surpass in influence a Napoleon breaking the world to his sway. And not only is their work higher in kind; who knows but that they are doing a greater work even as to extent of surface than the conqueror? Who knows but that the being whom they inspire with holy and disinterested principles may communicate himself to others; and that, by a spreading agency, of which they were the silent origin, improvements may spread through a nation, through the world?

It would be difficult to believe that the child received her name through mere chance. It would seem that her devoted grandmother, who had inherited a full measure of love, was strongly inspired when she named the child "Mary," a name which had implied love since the beginning of Christianity. One is ever conscious that Jesus' mother, Mary, was the embodiment of love. And the scriptures say that her devoted friend, Mary Magdalene, also possessed that divine quality. "It was that Mary which anointed and wiped His feet with her hair, whose brother Lazarus was sick." (John 11-2.) And here we are told "Now Jesus loved Martha and her sister (Mary), and Lazarus." (John 11-5.) Through God's love, Jesus was able to raise Lazarus from the dead, and here was a divine bond uniting Lazarus and his sisters with Jesus.

Above all, we are reminded of the sweetness of the name of the Virgin Mother.

In *The Glories of Mary* by St. Alphonsus de Liguori, we read, p. 260:

> The great name Mary, which was given to the divine mother, did not come to her from her parents, nor was it given to her by the mind or will of man, as is the case with all other names that are imposed in this world, but it came from heaven, and was given her by divine ordinance. This is attested by St. Jerome, St. Epiphamius, St. Antonimus, and others. "The name Mary came from the treasury of the divinity," says St. Peter Damien.

On page 262 of the same book, the author tells us:

> Abbot Francone speaking on this subject says, "There is no other name after the Son, in heaven or on earth, whence pious minds derive so much grace, hope and sweetness." After the most sacred name of Jesus, the name of Mary is so rich in every good thing, that on earth and in heaven there is no other from which devout souls receive so much grace, hope and sweetness.

It is a blessed spiritual heritage to bear the divine name Mary when the bearer is truly in tune with the Supreme Law. The world was to be shown that the newborn child at Bow would carry the name with understanding grace throughout her entire life.

Mary's grandmother was keenly conscious of the divine meaning of the name she conferred upon her grandchild, although she may not have been fully aware that one bearing that name may be subconsciously stimulated to reflect in life the virtue which the name implied, if suitable avenues are left open to divine expression.

Those avenues must be opened. It is not sufficient merely to possess the potentiality of love for it to be expressed in life. For while love is present in every person, it does not rise into activity in equal degrees in all of them. There are some people who inherently radiate love to a much greater degree than do others; they are the ones who have kept the door open to divine prompting and are in tune with Divinity. The less fortunate have had their intuitive powers dampened by habits of thought which adhere to the material side of life. Such people may possess splendid, upright qualities, lead exemplary lives, and adhere rigidly to religious teachings; yet God's love does not flow freely through them.

The reason for these differences in persons is not clearly traceable. Perhaps it is because

> All nature teaches God's love to man, but man cannot love God supremely and set his whole affections on spiritual things, while loving the material or trusting in it more than in the spiritual. We must forsake the foundation of material systems, however time-honored, if we would gain the Christ as our only Saviour. (*Science and Health*, pp. 326-8-9-14)

Under the title "New Commandment," she says in *Miscellaneous Writings*:

> The divinity of St. John's Gospel brings to view overwhelming tides of revelation, and its spirit is baptismal; he chronicles this teaching "A new commandment I give unto you, That ye love one another."

> Jesus who so loved the world that he gave his life (in the flesh) for it, saw that Love had a new commandment even for him. What was it?

> It must have been a rare revelation of infinite Love,

a new tone on the scale ascending, such as eternity is ever sounding. Could I impart to the student the higher sense I entertain of Love, it would partly illustrate the divine energy that brings to human weakness might and majesty. Divine Love eventually causes mortals to turn away from sepulchres of sin, and look no more into them as realities. It calls loudly on them to bury the dead out of sight; to forgive and forget whatever is unlike the risen, immortal Love; and to shut out all opposite sense. Christ enjoins it upon man to help those who know not what he is doing in their behalf, and therefore curse him; enjoins taking them by the hand and leading them, if possible, to Christ, by loving words and deeds. Charity thus serves as admonition and instruction, and works out the purpose of Love.

Mark Baker was a man whose inherent love was held within the limits of his religious orthodoxy. His orthodox religious leanings and practical resourcefulness as a provider and administrative leader fitted him to serve, not only as the head of a household, but as justice of the peace, deacon of the church, school committeeman, and chaplain of the State Militia. He was a man well-occupied in helping others and his activities were avenues for the expression of his love.

But through his Puritan ancestry he reflected an earnestness of purpose with rigid adherence to accepted codes. It is therefore understandable that it was difficult for him to accept fully his daughter's freer expression of God's love. His will was strong and not easy to swerve.

It is probable that her father's firmness was added to Mary's inherited virtues. This gave her the will to pursue her purpose under the many difficult circumstances encountered during her formative years and those which followed.

Mary's endowment, then, was a rich one. Further testimony on the importance of heritage is given by Paul in his Epistle to the Ephesians (11:5-11):

Having predestinated us into the adoption of children by Jesus Christ to himself, according to the good pleasure of his will,—In whom also we have obtained an inheritance, being predestinated according to the purpose of him who worketh all things after the counsel of his own will.

Sibyl Wilbur touches upon the subject of heredity in a rather adroit way. In *The Life of Mary Baker Eddy*, she says:

Though we instinctively give heredity and natural environment a close scrutiny and in viewing a character are prone to believe these to be the principal formative agents, we still fancy we behold how destiny strikes through circumstances and grasping a life drags it root and all from its soil and culture to replant it for its great development. We shall see how Love inspired Mary Baker and drew her tenderly out of Puritanism to fit her for leadership in warfare against materialism.

Aside from the heritage Mary received from her ancestry, there is another possible influence which should not be overlooked.

Her mother had a close friend named Sarah Gault. The two women met frequently, discussed religious matters and prayed aloud together. Of these meetings Hugh A. Studdert Kennedy, in his book entitled *Mrs. Eddy*, gives the following account, p. 14:

During these meetings, Mrs. Baker many times told her neighbor, Mrs. Gault, that she felt herself to be the most wicked woman, because of strange thoughts she had regarding her youngest child, which was yet unborn. She told Mrs. Gault that she could not keep her thoughts away from the strong conviction that the child was holy and consecrated and set apart for wonderful achievements, even before her birth. She said "I know these are sinful thoughts for me to entertain,

but I cannot shake them off." Then these two devout
women would talk the question over and pray.

There were recurring thoughts on the part of Abigail Baker
"that this child was holy and consecrated and set apart for wonderful achievements." The intuitions of Mary's mother were
keen, for she was devoutly religious and accustomed to commut-
ing with God. Nor was this revelation an isolated occurrence.
It was recurring and persistent, as evidenced by the remark
"she could not keep her thoughts away from the strong conviction."

Perception or discernment is often keen in those with truly
spiritual natures, for they are responsive to inward beckonings
and promptings.

The fact that Mrs. Baker was recognized as an intelligent,
talented woman and intensely practical in her household affairs prevails upon many to consider her revelation seriously and
in good faith. Previously she had brought other children into the
world and no mention is recorded of similar revelations. There
was no possibility of notional hysteria, for she was poised and
placid in her behavior, and so highly regarded in the community
that her judgment was sought on numerous occasions.

Thus it would seem that no ordinary happening was taking
place, that divine intuitive discernments were being received.
The prophecy which they conveyed came into full reality in later
years when Mary disclosed her discovery of Christian Science.

Men have long been conscious of an all-governing power,
of an all-pervading unity with God the Father, of a one Mind and
one intelligence. All creative thoughts come to man from a
supreme intelligence, with man serving as a vehicle for bringing that intelligence into expression. Every experience mani-
fested to man reaches him from an all-prevailing source because
he, man, forms part of the general scheme of being.

History has proved repeatedly that men are moved to do
great things by a power not their own. The influences which
prompt them may not always be well defined; they may appear
in manifold ways and sometimes may not be understood. Yet

there is effective response in many instances. Those who tell us they have received divine messages through vision of angels describe their visitations in the only manner left to them by human vocabulary.

There are a few well-known instances recorded in history in which men and women have been moved to serve a divine cause. For example, we learn that when Zacharias was standing at the altar, an angel appeared and informed him that his prayer had been heard and that his wife would bear a son and "thou shalt call his name John"; also, that an angel came to the Virgin Mary and told her "thou shalt conceive in thy womb, and bring forth a son and shalt call his name Jesus." When Saul was journeying to Damascus "he fell to earth and heard a voice saying unto him, 'Saul, Saul, why persecutest thou me?' " When Peter was imprisoned by Herod he prayed to God unceasingly and an angel appeared, saying, " 'Arise up quickly.' And his chains fell off from his hands" and he was freed to continue his great work of establishing the Christian Church. When King Darius committed Daniel to the lions' den and in the morning, finding him unhurt, spoke to him, Daniel replied, "My God hath sent His angel and hath shut the lions' mouths." Nor can we overlook Moses, who delivered the Israelites from the Egyptians, for in Exodus and Leviticus are recorded many messages received by Moses from the Lord and we can see how these messages guided him in numerous practical ways.

Saint Francis, the Apostle of Love, was greatly influenced by messages which he received, so much so that they diverted him from a life of luxury to one of poverty. Early in his reformed career, when he was in the habit of visiting the little church of San Damian in the fields just below Assisi and at a time when he was deeply absorbed in prayer, he heard a voice saying: "Francis, do you not see that my house is in ruins? Go and restore it for me."

History tells us how diligently and self-sacrificingly he did his Master's bidding, under the most difficult circumstances. When the little church of San Damian had been restored, he proceeded to restore many other churches needing similar repairs.

The life of Saint Theresa, who lived in the sixteenth century, was no less remarkable than was that of Saint Francis. She too was born in the lap of luxury and at an early age entered a Carmelite convent. Her stay there was intermittent, owing to severe illnesses. Many of her hours there were spent alone and she told her confessor that she received recurring messages from the Lord. The church authorities would not believe her and charged her with heresy. She was distrusted by everyone, and demands were made that she be delivered into the hands of the Inquisition.

Her road became increasingly difficult. But she reported that the Lord had appeared to her and said: "Be not afraid, my daughter. I shall not abandon you." Yet the world continued to suspect her and she was called a liar. Finally, after an exceedingly strict and rigid investigation by holy men, her honesty was acknowledged and it was decided to tolerate and accept the visionary nun.

Theresa was saddened because the life and conduct within the Carmelite convent no longer adhered to the simple and frugal rules of the ancient order. The convent was now courting a life of ease and condoned the reception of visitors on a social scale from outside its domain. Theresa was influenced by the voices she heard to remedy this lax condition which prevailed in all Carmelite convents and monasteries. There was great opposition to her efforts and numerous measures were taken to obstruct her work of establishing new convents whose inmates would practice the pious lives of the ancestral order. But her unwavering perseverance rewarded her during the last twenty years of her life. This purposeful woman untiringly engaged in the reform of her order and established seventeen new convents. No better evidence can be found of a practical person being moved to accomplishment in the physical world through messages divinely received than that given by the life and work of Saint Theresa.

Contemporaneously with Mary Baker Eddy, there lived another famous woman, Elizabeth Blackwell, who was born in the same year and who, after an eventful and useful life, died in the same year. Elizabeth Blackwell had the feeling that God was directing her life. She was moved to follow a medical career although she met with the utmost opposition when seeking entry as a student to medical schools. At last she was admitted to Geneva College and graduated at the head of her class.

But hostility to her aim continued and many difficulties were placed in her way, to such an extent that she could not find a respectable boarding house willing to let a female doctor's shingle be shown on the premises. When a proposal of marriage was made to her, she rejected it. She believed that God was directing her to open medical careers for women. In her diary she wrote: "Because of the stern life I have chosen, all thoughts of love and marriage must be put aside." Finally, success came to her and in consequence of her untiring work, the medical profession was opened to women the world over. Besides this great stride, other reforms in the profession were instituted because Elizabeth Blackwell was convinced that sunlight, good food, uncontaminated milk, fresh air and pure water would prevent and help cure many illnesses.

History affords countless other examples of persons being divinely influenced by messages coming to them in one form or another. The hearing of a spoken voice or the reception of a vision is not uncommon. Then there is also the intuitive influence that comes without voice or vision, yet is given effective interpretation. In the light of these very real phenomena which have so frequently been associated with important events, one is moved to take the occurrences connected with Mary Baker Eddy's birth seriously.

In *Science and Health*, pp. 298-299, she wrote:

> Angels are not etherealized human beings, evolving animal qualities in their wings; but they are celestial visitants, flying on spiritual, not material, pinions. Angels are pure thoughts from God, winged with

Truth and Love, no matter what their individualism
may be.

My angels are exalted thoughts, appearing at the
door of some sepulchre, in which human belief has
buried its fondest earthly hopes. With white fingers
they point upward to new and glorious trust, to higher
ideals of life and its joys. Angels are God's representatives. These upward-soaring beings never lead towards
self, sin, or materiality, but guide to the divine Principle of all good, whither every real individuality, image,
or likeness of God, gathers. By giving earnest heed to
these spiritual guides they tarry with us, and we entertain "angels unawares."

CHAPTER

2

Mary's babyhood was spent largely in her grandmother's care. This deeply pious and loving woman was ideally fitted to mold the early life of the one who was to grow up in the work of Christ and who was to give Christian Science to the world. It is during the years of babyhood that impressions become indelibly registered on the developing mind. Thus with the heritage Mary had received from her especially favorable ancestry, she was particularly susceptible to an evolutionary awakening in the spirit of love. Her deeply religious mother, always conscious that her child had been brought into the world for "wonderful achievement," added her devotion to that given by the grandmother. The child, most certainly, lived in an atmosphere of piety and love.

One cannot but help regard such influences seriously. It has long been recognized that heritage and environment are real forces in shaping the mind, etching deeply on the consciousness influences which have distinct bearings on personality, character, and the outcome of a person's whole life. Heartfelt belief in a noble cause paves the way toward noble realities and efforts which become devoted to their promotion. The underlying spiritual foundation given to Mary during her formative years endowed her with a firm belief in God's love for His children. This belief she fostered deep down in her soul, and as was to be seen in later years, a virtue combining love, patience, kindness and sympathy was welded within her. These God-given qualities became pre-eminently outstanding throughout her life.

Little has been recorded about Mary's childhood. There really appeared no reason for any especial recording of it at the time. While it is true that Abigail Baker had had a prenatal conviction that her child was holy and consecrated, yet this early impression did not cause her to record chronologically the life of the growing child.

The farm on which Mary lived was a busy place from early morning till night. Her mother and sisters worked long hours at their many household duties, which included house-cleaning, cooking, washing, sewing, weaving, preserving, and other chores that were so necessary in those days. Her father and brothers attended to the more strenuous side of farm life, cultivating the ground, tending the cattle, clearing new areas by removing logs and rocks, repairing equipment, fences and buildings, and providing firewood.

In such a busy homestead there was neither the time nor the opportunity to reflect that future generations might desire to know something about the early life of the youngest child.

As a child, Mary was happy and well loved by all members of the family. From an early age she was attentive to the conversations within her hearing. Her family soon became aware that no talk was really beyond her understanding and that she liked best to listen to discussions on the weightier subjects, especially when they touched upon the welfare of someone she liked.

Because Mary's father was highly regarded in the community and took an active part in its civic and religious affairs, the Baker homestead frequently served as a meeting place where prominent people gathered and earnestly debated a wide variety of subjects. Farmers, politicians, businessmen and clergymen were among those who received the hospitality of the Baker home. They brought their problems for discussion and clarification, for it was generally recognized that Mark Baker possessed a goodly amount of practical common sense. Even disputes were brought to him for settlement.

These meetings gave young Mary a golden opportunity to absorb freely many subjects from many angles. Her keen mind was cross-fertilized with a variety of worthwhile material for, as we already have noted, she paid close and understanding attention to all discussions which took place in her presence. The pros and cons of the subjects under discussion were no doubt freely aired before her, and must have awakened in her a realization that there is usually more than one side to a question. One progresses by observing and weighing conversations within hearing. These become great teachers to discerning listeners such as was Mary.

Her own opinions evidently took form in those early days for, as was to be seen later, she was quite sure of her own beliefs, even when they were contrary to those which were generally accepted by her elders. She possessed resolution, a quality which remained with her throughout her life. It was this impelling force that held her from swerving from her own inborn convictions. Without this God-given attribute, Mary would have been unable to overcome the many difficulties which were in her path for so many years. With her resolution were linked the high ideals that permeated her mind when, as a child, she unconsciously analyzed the debates she overheard.

The frequent visits of clergymen to the Baker home were a source of special interest to Mary and no doubt aided in her theological enlightenment. She was particularly sensitive to the religious atmosphere lent by these visits, which consequently must have contributed in some measure to the formation of her spiritual growth. A similar influence was felt in the childhood of that great reformer, Martin Luther. Barnas Sears, in his *The Life of Luther*, says:

> An early writer states, that he had heard from relations of Luther at Mansfield, that the father was often known to pray earnestly at the bedside of his son, that God would bless him and make him useful. Mathesius says, that Luther's father, not only for his own gratification, but especially for the benefit of his son, frequently invited the clergymen and school-teachers of the place to his house. Thus were domestic influences brought to aid, in every suitable way, to form a taste for moral

and intellectual culture. This is what Monica did for Augustine; Arethusa for Chrysostom, and Basil's and Gregory Nazianzen's parents for them, and, through them, for the world.

In reviewing Mary's early development we should take notice of her convictions because heartfelt beliefs do so much in molding a person's character. We already have noted that Mary possessed an inherent love for all of God's children and creatures. It was love that served as a basis for her beliefs and which she fostered deeply in her soul. These convictions, catalyzed by love, developed in her a resolution which enabled her to steer a true course in the great work that was to be hers. It was resolution which stimulated action all along the path of her endeavor and brought to the surface the impelling force inherent in the universe. Without this force, her work could never have been brought to fruition.

It was resolution which impelled the self-discipline so evidently practiced by Mary at an early age. Having acquired the habit so early in life, she did not find it irksome in later years when there became a great need for patience, forbearance and self-control. It was resolution which caused Mary to cling to the path of integrity during periods of adversity when there were merciless onslaughts upon her beliefs and teachings. Throughout these trials she always remained true to the high principles she so firmly believed in. Her honest opinions were not to be diluted.

It is evident that Mary was an astute student during her early childhood, and that her curriculum was exceedingly broad since it consisted of the many subjects which came under discussion by adults who were intellectually well above the average. Thus, her reasoning faculty was developed far beyond that of the average child of equal age. The power of discrimination associated with reasoning aided her in evolving her own thoughts and opinions. These became well formed in the child's mind and must have aided her in simplifying her understanding of truth and Christian teachings.

Because Mary's health was delicate from birth, her school attendance was not very regular. The noise, confinement and severe routine of the overcrowded country school which she and her sisters attended did not agree with her, and it was deemed advisable, by the doctor whom Mr. Baker consulted, to keep Mary away from school as much as possible and let her exercise out-of-doors. Mary's mental development was regarded by the doctor to be in advance of her years and constitution. The family followed his advice and, accordingly, from an early age until she was fifteen or more, she continued her education at home.

No doubt this was the best thing that could have happened, because we have already noted Mary's propensity for acquiring knowledge by listening to the conversation of adults and observing her surroundings. With Mary's proclivities, there could not have been a more suitable educational course during her youthful years than that which she pursued at home. It might even seem that divine guidance was effective in this decision.

Remaining at home gave Mary greater opportunities to come under the tender and sympathetic influence of her mother. Mrs. Baker was especially suited to aid her child in her religious education because, as the daughter of Deacon Nathaniel Ambrose of Pembroke, a pillar of the Congregational Church, she undoubtedly had acquired a thorough familiarity with the Holy Bible.

On several occasions Mary had heard her mother's voice calling her and upon going to her mother in response, learned that she had not been called. One evening before Mary went to bed, her mother read the story of Samuel to her and told her, should she hear the voice again, to answer as Samuel had done: "Speak, Lord, for thy servant heareth."

When Mary's aged grandmother passed out of the home scene, the close companionship between mother and daughter grew even stronger, and Mary came to regard her mother as a saintly woman. This reverence she held throughout her life. Sibyl Wilbur in *The Life of Mary Baker Eddy* tells us:

> After her death (referring to Mary's mother) the clergyman, the Rev. Richard S. Rust, D.D., who, Mrs. Eddy has said, "Knew my sainted mother in all the

walks of life" wrote of her as one who possessed a presence which made itself felt like gentle dew and cheerful light.

Mary enjoyed reading and studying alone and the Bible became her constant companion. Remaining at home without a regular school routine afforded her the freedom to follow her own natural inclinations. Her time was her own to be used as best suited her. Many happy moments were spent with her mother, who liked to help her daughter in her Bible and other studies. She read many books and newspapers, with remarkable understanding. There were ample moments for meditation and for prayer. Both formed important parts in building wisdom and in preparing Mary for the Christian work that later became hers to do.

Leisure renders meditation and concentration possible. It provides an atmosphere of hospitality which sets the mind at ease and permits it to explore the highways and byways of thought, drawing upon memory and experience as material for constructive and harmonious regimentation of the influences of environment. Nothing worthwhile can be achieved without meditation, and meditation is severely hampered without leisure and repose.

Mary Baker put her leisure to use. Her environment was fertile and well suited to her needs. She cached away in her memory all that was beneficent and, as time passed, she progressively organized and marshalled her experiences to serve mankind. Strong and sensitive natures are gifted with wonderful precocity, effervescing in early life and prophetically projecting into future achievements.

If we look into the lives of those people who have contributed much to mankind, we will find that the time they took for meditation was an essential element in preparing them for tasks to come, even though such intervals for meditation were of short duration and interlaced with activity. We know that Abraham Lincoln in his boyhood worked hard as a farm laborer. Yet he took time off to loll under a tree or in a cabin loft where he could leisurely study and meditate. In this way, the Great Emancipator prepared himself for the duties which later were to be placed on his shoulders and which he rose to fulfill so devotedly.

In the autobiographies of many people whose achievements served most the needs and aims of the world, we find the claim that solitude is the prerequisite of constructive thinking. Solitude leaves the avenue open for divine guidance. Great religious leaders recognize this and invariably resort to intervals of quiet relaxation, permitting themselves to be responsive to the divine law.

It is at such times that the great truths have been revealed to man. During a period of relaxation St. John, The Divine, received the Revelation. "I John, who also am your brother, and companion in tribulation, and in the kingdom and patience of Jesus Christ, was in the isle that is called Patmos for the word of God, and for the testimony of Jesus Christ. I was in the Spirit on the Lord's day, and heard behind me a great voice, as of a trumpet." John was "in the Spirit on the Lord's day"; he was in a period of relaxation, in communion with his Creator. He was a good servant of the Lord and listened well.

Mary's education was further advanced through the efforts of her brother Albert, who was eleven years her senior. He was extremely fond of his youngest sister, as she was of him.

Talking to his mother one day, he said, "Mother, Mary is as beautiful as an angel."

"Well, my son," she replied, "she is as gentle and sweet-tempered as one."

Thus there was a unity in the expression of those sentiments by three living souls, each full of appreciation of the love which the good Lord had given them, each full of appreciation of the innate good which filled the hearts of the others. One should be ever grateful for an atmosphere so sublime that it became indelibly impressed in Mary's soul and served to stimulate her inherent love through all future years.

Besides the help her mother and her brother Albert gave, other members of the household assisted Mary in her lessons, and several ministers who visited the family frequently aided Mary in the subjects closest to her heart. All in all, the tutelage she received was well suited to her temperament, and she absorbed a fund of knowledge of her own choosing.

She had learned to read from the Bible and from Lindley Murray's Reader. In so doing, her religious and philosophical leanings were stimulated to study further in these subjects. She had no difficulty in reading serious subjects with understanding, and her memory was so keen she was able to retain indefinitely all she had learned. She became a fluent reader and frequently read newspapers aloud to her family. Not only did she become familiar with her Lindley Murray, but also with her Westminster Catechism, which she would repeat each Sunday.

The help her brother Albert gave was of an advanced order for one as young as Mary. Albert was a brilliant student and stood high in his studies at Dartmouth. He was to become one of the ablest lawyers of New Hampshire and a close friend of Franklin Pierce, governor of the state and later President of the United States. After graduating from college, Albert became a law partner of Franklin Pierce and a member of the New Hampshire State Legislature where he worked for better laws. He was, therefore, a most valuable guide and mentor for the young Mary, with her keen mentality and spiritual nature.

When Albert was home from Dartmouth on his first vacation, Mary told him one day, "And I want very much to be a scholar, too."

"A scholar; and why, little sister?"

"Because when I grow up I shall write a book; and I must be wise to do it. I must be as great a scholar as you or Mr. Franklin Pierce. Already I have read Young's *Night Thoughts,* and I understand it."

"Well, sister," said Albert seriously, "we will have this for a secret and I will teach you. You are still a very little girl, you know; but study your grammar and my Latin grammar. Next summer when I am home I will teach you to read Latin. Does that make you happy?" (Sibyl Wilbur, *The Life of Mary Baker Eddy.*)

Albert was true to his word and during his vacation periods, for the remainder of his college days, he devoted much time to

Mary. During those years they read moral science and natural philosophy together and studied the Latin, Greek and Hebrew grammars. An exchange of thoughts upon spiritual matters, no doubt, was liberally interwoven with other studies.

The sympathetic bond between brother and sister, indeed, was spiritual as well as intellectual. In their thoughts resided purity; a desire to serve others; a wish to be always true to their Creator. Nor was this a fleeting sentiment. Rather this profound urge to prepare themselves for the duties the future would bring was recognized by them as one which demanded self-imposed labor in quest of self-improvement without self-gain. Each was an inspiration to the other—an inspiration which became indelibly registered in depths of their souls. Character, already of a high order, was being improved and refined to an ever-increasing purity. God's true love was felt to be within their hearts and was being exercised in a spirit of benevolence.

In this picture there is also the spirit of self-conquest, sought via paths of truth leading to perfection in understanding, self-control, and self-effacement. Mary and Albert, clearly, were not concerned with thoughts of self-gain but only with those which would best serve the world.

Because when I grow up I shall write a book; and I must be wise to do it. That this was a true prophecy was certainly proven later. It was not an idle gesture, nor a childish whim; it was not a mere ambition. It was a resolve. There was a mission to be performed, a mission which had not as yet been clearly patterned in the child's mind. It was a step in the evolution which would progressively unfold into a clear picture of Christian teaching. It was not spontaneous. Mary came into the world endowed with the spirit of love; a love which would grow as she grew and which would seek expression in the practical avenues of life. Formative steps had accompanied her from babyhood to childhood, and now a sufficient degree of wisdom had become hers to impel the desire for further preparation.

I must be wise to do it. The statement in itself expresses a high degree of wisdom. There was work to be done, and done well.

Only one especially equipped would be able to give the world a book worthy of its mission.

It should be noted that Mary did not express a desire to write a book; she distinctly said: "I shall write a book." The statement was positive and left no doubt as to her meaning. She knew she must prepare herself for the task, and confided her determination to her brother who was in such close rapport with her.

There was within Mary's consciousness a union with divinity, a consciousness that she was human and could only express herself in human ways and with the use of tools used by human beings. She must fit herself accordingly. She must possess the right tools. She did not say she should or would like to be wise but emphasized, "I *must* be wise to do it." She decreed the course she felt she *must* pursue, and her words left no doubt as to the meaning she wished to convey.

Mary was nine years old when her brother Albert entered Dartmouth and thirteen when he graduated. During these years, while home on vacation periods, Albert continued to aid her in her studies. She made steady progress in her education, for she was continually at her books. The Bible, which she studied constantly, was her close companion, and she became well versed in its teachings. She took her religion seriously, formed very definite opinions from what she learned and could not be diverted from them.

In New England homes in those days it was quite usual for religion to form the important topic of conversation. Mary's views were beginning to cause grave concern to her father. God's love for all His children had become a principle in Mary's thinking which she applied in its fullest meaning. Love was naturally in her heart; therefore, she was readily able to visualize its implication in many passages in both the Old and the New Testaments. She could not recognize a wrathful God who would punish His children. Hatred and punishment did not conform with her convictions and were things to be avoided. One's own sins were to be corrected through repentance and by avoiding repetition. They could not be overcome by wounds inflicted by a relentless master.

Mark Baker, accepting the full teaching of Calvin as to God, Heaven and Hell, naturally expected his children to hew to the strict lines of his beliefs. It was a blow to him when he became aware of the strange ways of his youngest child, the child so dear to his heart. The "voices" she had heard calling her he could attribute to the child's delicate health, but how could he condone her inability to accept the religious dogma which was so firmly inbred in him?

The story of Mary's difficulties with her father, told so adroitly and sympathetically by Sibyl Wilbur in *The Life of Mary Baker Eddy*, is quoted here:

> Her religious experience reached a grave crisis when she was twelve years of age, though she did not unite with the church until five years later at Sanbornton Bridge. While still at Bow, writing and studying, her father's relentless theology was alarmed at her frequent expressions of confidence in God's love. He held to a hard and bitter doctrine of predestination and believed that a horrible decree of endless punishment awaited sinners on a final judgment day.
>
> Whether it was logic and moral science taught her by her brother, or the trusting love instilled by her mother who guided her to yield herself to the voice of God within her, Mary resisted her father on the matter of "unconditional election." Beautiful in her serenity and immovable in her faith, the daughter sat before the stern father of the iron will. His sires had signed a covenant in blood and would he not wrestle with this child who dared the wrath of God?
>
> And well he did wrestle and the home was filled with his torrents and emotion. But though Mary might have quoted to him her own baby speech, she was too respectful and his "vociferations" went unrebuked. It is a remarkable thing to note, the conscience of a

child in defense of its faith. Can anyone suppose it an easy thing to resist a father so convicted with belief in dogma, a father, too, whom all their world honored and heeded. We may be sure it was not easy; that, indeed, to do so tortured this little girl's heart. But Mark Baker was acting according to his conscience, and the child knew it and respected him. She did not view this struggle of consciences as a quarrel, and repudiated all her life the idea that she ever quarreled with her father.

The paragraphs above quoted give an intimate picture of the difficulties which beset Mary and her father in their religious understandings. Truly, much sympathy is due Mark Baker. He was firm in his beliefs and found it impossible to alter them. To him, it would be sacrilege to do so, for was not this dogma handed down by his forefathers; had he not been diligently schooled in it from early childhood; were not the ministers of the church to which he belonged of the same belief? There could be no stronger reasons than these for his firm adherence to his beliefs and for denying his child's as true. What authority had been given her to hold a belief that was at variance with his own, one which was so firmly ingrained in him and in the members of his church? How could a child so young, who had hardly left the doors of her home, think differently than her parents?

It was a heartbreaking matter for Mark Baker. Sincerity and determination were his strong points; duty to his family and to society had been diligently fulfilled. How could he permit this child of his own blood to go astray? Firmness was necessary; it was a duty he owed the child he loved so dearly; she must not be allowed to go astray in a matter as important as religion. No wonder "the home was filled with his torrents and emotion." The poor man was beside himself!

It was these qualities which did so much to hold Mary to a true course, one from which she could not be diverted, even by the earnest and forceful pleas of the father she respected so much. It was these qualities, coupled with tolerance, patience, kindness, humility and God's love, that gave her the understanding which assured her, in her heart, that there was no quarrel between her and her father.

No, it was not a quarrel; it was a matter of two distinct differences of opinion, expressed with reverent solemnity on the one hand and, on the other, forcefully and emotionally. With two minds so sure of their own opinions, how was it possible to reach a compromise? We have seen that it was not possible. This situation, while an unhappy one for both, benefited Mary because the challenge must have caused her to search deep down in her heart for the truth. Was it possible that her father, who was so sure of his position, could be right and she wrong? Such a student would weigh the subject in every way. She no doubt did so, for it was not possible for her to study her Bible, as she so constantly did, without having uppermost in her mind her father's understanding of God. As passages in her Bible came under her notice which she considered as related to the differences in understanding, she naturally would scrutinize them closely to see if they in any way revealed a meaning different from that which she had so firmly and fervently evolved in her young mind. Judging by Mary's reiterated beliefs in subsequent years, she must have found no reason to alter her understanding of God—God full of love for His children, God without wrath.

The controversies over religion, which so severely tried her faith and led her to review again and again the Book she so cherished, must have done much to clarify her understanding of the Holy Scriptures and to convince her that she was right and her father wrong. There had been no doubt in her mind previously, concerning the verity of her beliefs, and now these beliefs had been confirmed by the further studies which dissension had demanded. Mary Baker was greatly strengthened in consequence and was moved more than ever to adhere to her life's purpose.

Through these long periods of trial, it was important that Mary had the deep love of her mother, who had encouraged her "to yield herself to the voice of God within her." Her love and sympathy must have been a source of great help and comfort to the child, and did much to stimulate in her God's love, so inherently hers and which she expressed in so many ways. Her mother's love brought ready response of the kind, infusing devotion to both mother and father.

Even before the death of her grandmother, Mary's love had found expression in her sympathy for dumb creatures, knowing that God cared for them all. She concerned herself with the comfort of the animals on the farm, wondering whether they were warm and comfortable on winter nights and feeling distressed if she thought they were not. One November evening her brother found her huddled by the pig pen, singing softly to the squealing pigs. She had left her warm fireside to comfort the poor pigs so they would go to sleep. Her brother carried her home to their grandmother, laughingly telling her of the lullaby by the pigsty. Mary exclaimed in all seriousness, "But they are crying and it must be because it is cold and dark out there."

This simple story is an excellent illustration of Mary's conscious love for God's creatures. None was too lowly to receive her sympathy and help. While this trait is not uncommon in children, it was especially outstanding in Mary. Her sensitive nature responded freely to the promptings she felt within her to serve all who needed her love.

She remained faithful as ever to her studies, and her Bible remained constantly with her. But the determined opposition of her father to her religious views had a serious effect on his frail child. The doctor found she had a fever and commended her to the care of her mother, suggesting that Mr. Baker cease his opposition. Referring to this incident in later years in *R and S*, Mary wrote:

My mother, as she bathed my burning temples, bade me lean on God's love, which would give me rest, if I went to Him in prayer, as I was wont to do, seeking His guidance. I prayed; and a soft glow of ineffable joy came over me. The fever was gone, and I rose and dressed myself, in a normal condition of health; my mother saw this and was glad. The physician marvelled; and the "horrible decree" of predestination—as John Calvin rightly called his own tenet—forever lost its power over me.

Here again we see love intertwined in Mary's thinking. Her mother knew how fervently her daughter regarded God's love and understood what peace of mind would be given her child if she bade her to "lean on God's love." Mary prayed to God for guidance as her mother advised. She must have done this with all the earnestness in her heart, for the fever left her and the "horrible decree of predestination forever lost its power" over her. She prayed as she "was wont to do, seeking His guidance." Praying, she knew that God would hear her, and He did. She recognized her reward for her trueness of heart, for had not God freed her of the torment of John Calvin's "own tenet"?

This experience served, incidentally, as an example of the efficacy of prayer, and she felt an awareness of the revelation which later became so evident. Every instance of the kind builds increasing faith and stimulates reliance upon the beneficent resource.

Accordingly, an important stride had been made in her spiritual ascendancy. What at the time may have seemed like unfortunate occurrences in family life were, indeed, the opposite. Actually, they served as foundation stones upon which the strong structure of Christian Science was to be built. The hand of Providence was at work.

It was at this time that Mary, who was now twelve years of age, was examined by the pastor of the Congregational Church to which her parents had belonged for half a century. However, she did not unite with the church until she was seventeen years of age. As we have seen, the doctrine of unconditional election and predestination had been troubling her greatly, and the young girl was sorely tried when the meeting was held for the examination of candidates for membership. Of this meeting, she writes in *Retrospection and Introspection:*

> The pastor was an old-school expounder of the strictest Presbyterian doctrines. He was apparently as eager to have unbelievers in these dogmas lost, as he was to have elect believers converted and rescued from perdition; for both salvation and condemnation depended, according to his views, upon the good pleasure of infinite Love. However, I was ready for his doleful questions, which I answered without tremor, declaring that never could I unite with the church, if assent to this doctrine was essential thereto.
>
> Distinctly do I recall what followed. I stoutly maintained that I was willing to trust God, and take my chance of spiritual safety with my brothers and sisters —not one of whom had then made any profession of religion—even if my creedal doubts left me outside the doors. The minister then wished me to tell him when I had experienced a change of heart; but tearfully I had to respond that I could not designate any precise time. Nevertheless he persisted in the assertion that I *had* been truly regenerated, and asked me to say how I felt when the new light dawned within me. I replied that I could only answer him in words of the Psalmist: "Search me, O God, and know my heart: try me, and know my thoughts: and see if there be any wicked way in me, and lead me in the way everlasting."

Mary was only twelve years of age when she spoke these words. Yet her clarity of thought on the subject of religion was equal to that of a highly intelligent person of mature years who had thoroughly searched the subject and weighed it carefully. She was sure of her ground, sure of herself, and sure she was divinely guided. She was aware of the narrowness in her pastor's point of view and was unwilling to follow in the same erroneous path. She must have been conscious that some day or other this error in the interpretation of God's teachings would be corrected and that a true understanding would become universally accepted, that "infinite love" cannot harmonize with hell and damnation, but that God is love and is always kind. For did not God's Son tell us:

> As the Father hath loved me, so have I loved you: continue ye in my love.

> If ye keep my commandments, ye shall abide in my love; even as I have kept my Father's commandments, and abide in His love.

> These things have I spoken unto you, that my joy might remain in you, and that your joy might be full.

> This is my commandment: That ye love one another, as I have loved you.

> Greater love hath no man than this: that a man lay down his life for his friends.

> (John 15:9-13)

> Be ye therefore merciful, as your Father also is merciful.

> (Luke 6:36)

These quotations were surely uppermost in Mary's mind to give her fortitude in obeying "This is my commandment." How could the child do otherwise? For she recognized God's word as truth: "Sanctify them through thy truth; thy word is truth."

(John 17:17)

In this narration which Mary has given of her experience, there is to be seen not only a firmness of opinion but a meekness of heart, for she "tearfully" gave her response to her pastor when he persisted in ascertaining when she had been regenerated and how she felt when the new light dawned within her. Here is seen in Mary a true child of God. James Hamilton has said:

Meekness is the grace which, from beneath God's footstool, lifts up a candid and confiding eye, accepting God's smile of Fatherly affection, and adoring those perfections it cannot comprehend.

Mary's answer could not have been more appropriate, and it could not have entered the child's mind had she not been well versed in her Bible, and brimming over with meekness, love and contrition. Mary felt the need of God's own measure of her faith and yearned to be led "in the way everlasting." She could not relinquish the faith so lovingly bestowed upon her heart. She was willing to trust her spiritual safety with God.

It is difficult to find in history any other child as young as Mary was at this time who discerned, with such clarity, the spiritual truths taught in the Bible. Her faith did not then, and did not later, rest on any insecure foundation. People might disagree with her, but they could not weaken her faith in the principles she understood so well. Her premise was unassailable and unsuccessfully challenged. She was wise enough to know that it was for her alone to determine how and what she should think, that it was her privilege to do so, and that if she did not exercise this control over self, she would be untrue to divine guidance. Her triumph was complete because her heart and intellect were attuned to infinite virtue. This was conducive to thinking logically and sequentially along a fixed path leading to one's purpose in life.

Mary, conscious of the soundness of her knowledge of God's law, was so fortified and poised that she was always patient with those who opposed her way of thinking. She did not resent her pastor's efforts to change her mind, because she realized that his point of view, although unsound, was directed to correct what he believed to be an error in his candidate. In her self-possession, Mary had the strength to be generous toward her pastor, free of all bitterness and full of forgiveness.

Except for her understanding mother and sympathetic brother Albert, Mary's heart was a lonely one. She felt alone in her communion with God's love, the path through which she gained so much comfort. And there was so much more to learn; the question of healing had not been solved, although examples had been witnessed in which prayers had been answered, as when her mother bade her to lean on God's love and go to Him in prayer.

But people were not, at the time, being healed as they had been in early Christian days. There was some reason for this, which must be brought to light.

A contrite heart lends strength of purpose, also produces fertile soil favoring abundant growth of moral lessons which come its way, inducing sincere thoughts that unfold into realistic convictions. Beliefs about God, Jesus, the Bible, love and self-duty, all become positive in every sense. Thus, the way opens to progressive advances leading to the ultimate goal of perfection.

Although Mary's pastor became reconciled to leaving her to her own beliefs, she still suffered anguish by reason of her father's recurring arguments. He was not satisfied to leave his child to her own opinions because he still felt that she should be converted to the dogma he believed in. In consequence of the resulting tension, Mary was threatened with another nervous illness, so her mother thought it best to send her to visit a friend in the suburbs of Boston under the care of her brother Samuel. Her surroundings were pleasant, her hosts friendly, and efforts were made to interest her in new diversions.

The entertainments Mary shared and enjoyed during this visit did not free her of those thoughts which always were uppermost in her mind. Her love of nature and her love of all God's works, mingled with the lingering memory of unhappy moments with her father, moved her, during this visit, to write the expressive poem entitled *The Country-Seat* which is given here:

> Wild spirit of song,—midst the zephyrs at play
> In bowers of beauty,—I bend to thy lay,
> And woo, while I worship in deep sylvan spot,
> The Muses' soft echoes to kindle the grot.

Wake chords of my lyre, with musical kiss,
To vibrate and tremble with accents of bliss.

Here morning peers out, from her crimson repose,
On proud Prairie Queen and the modest Moss-rose;
And vesper reclines—when the dewdrop is shed
On the heart of the pink—in its odorous bed;
But Flora has stolen the rainbow and sky,
To sprinkle the flowers with exquisite dye.

Here fame-honored hickory rears his bold form,
And bares a brave breast to the lightning and storm,
While palm, bay, and laurel, in classical glee,
Chase tulip, magnolia, and fragrant fringe-tree;
And sturdy horse-chestnut for centuries hath given
Its feathery blossom and branches to heaven.

Here is life! Here is youth! Here the poet's world-wish,
Cool waters at play with the gold-gleaming fish;
While cactus a mellower glory receives
From light colored softly by blossom and leaves;
And nestling alder is whispering low,
In lap of the pear-tree, with musical flow.

Dark sentinel hedgerow is guarding repose,
Midst grotto and songlet and streamlet that flows
Where beauty and perfume from buds burst away,
And ope their closed cells to the bright, laughing day;
Yet, dwellers in Eden, earth yields you her tear,—
Oft plucked for the banquet, but laid on the bier.

Earth's beauty and glory delude as the shrine
Or fount of real joy and of visions divine;
But hope, as the eaglet that spurneth the sod,
May soar above matter, to fasten on God,
And freely adore all His spirit hath made,
Where rapture and radiance and glory ne'er fade.

Oh, give me the spot where affection may dwell
In sacred communion with home's magic spell!

Where flowers of feeling are fragrant and fair,
And those we most love find a happiness rare;
But clouds are a presage,—they darken my lay:
This life is a shadow, and hastens away.

(Retrospection and Introspection, pp. 17-18)

One cannot help but associate the tender thoughts in these lines with their author. Such appreciation of nature's gifts could flow only from one keenly responsive to God's love. As a guest among good friends who were conscientiously providing diverse social entertainments for her, she could not very well intrude subjects which were of greater interest to her and which remained pent up awaiting their release. Although she freely participated in the fun provided by her friends, Mary was far from unconscious of nature's beauties which surrounded her.

The wind bloweth where it listeth, and thou hearest the sound thereof, but canst tell whence it cometh, and whither it goeth: so is every one that is born of Spirit.   (John 3:8)

Mary must have been conscious of what she had so thoroughly learned from her Bible. Therefore, when in nature's garden, she breathed the sacred spirit which was all-pervading.

How much more interesting these companions of the garden were, to one so sensitive to nature's gifts, than were the happenings of the social parties which Mary attended. In moments of release from the frivolities of life, she could muse "And freely adore all His spirit hath made," and yearn "Oh, give me the spot where affection may dwell."

It is fortunate that this poem was preserved, for it reflects clearly the sanctity of Mary's thoughts, and shows how masterfully she was able to express them.

It must be remembered that this poem was written when she was still a child and at a time when she was away from home and temporarily released from the strain caused by her father's insistence that she alter her religious views. With the knowledge of the circumstances which presaged this poem, it becomes

possible to glean the full meaning Mary expressed so beautifully and with so much love. In the closing lines she is fervently
pleading for a "spot" of understanding with her father which
would restore her to a place in his affections; thus the darkening
clouds would fade away. Although her heart had been badly
bruised by the opposition she had encountered, nevertheless
it remained bathed in love which nothing could expunge.

The noted theologian and scientist Henry Drummond has
called love "The Greatest Thing in the World." Under that
title he lectured in part:

> Everyone has asked himself the great question of
> antiquity as of the modern world: What is the sum-
> mum bonum—the supreme good? You have life before
> you. Once only you can live it. What is the noblest
> object of desire, the supreme gift to covet?
>
> We have been accustomed to be told that the greatest
> thing in the religious world is Faith. That great word
> has been the key-note for centuries of the popular
> religion; and we have easily learned to look upon it
> as the greatest thing in the world. Well, we are wrong.
> If we have been told that, we may miss the mark. I
> have taken you in the chapter I have just read, to
> Christianity at its source; and there we have seen
> "The greatest of these is love." It is not an oversight.
> Paul was speaking of faith just a moment before. He
> says, "If I have all faith, so that I can remove moun-
> tains, and have not love, I am nothing." So far from
> forgetting he deliberately contrasts them, "Now abideth
> Faith, Hope, Love," and without a moment's hesitation
> the decision falls, "The greatest of these is Love!"

The greatest thing in Mary's heart was love.

During the next two or three years, she pursued her
studies at home as usual and took part in household duties and
family affairs. She enjoyed sociability and readily joined in
conversations which afforded an outlet for her exuberance. In
1832, her brother Samuel married a young Concord lady,

Eliza Glover. The wedding was a festive occasion and many friends of both families attended. Samuel, who by then was a successful building contractor in Boston, had come to Concord for the ceremony. The bride's brother George was there; he was a gay companion and did much merry-making in which Mary joined happily. The two became quite friendly.

Young George Glover was going to accompany Samuel and Eliza to Boston, where he planned to learn the building business under the guiding hand of his new brother-in-law. When he was leaving the family gathering, he laughingly lifted Mary up and told her he would be back in five years to marry her. In later years he proved his sincerity.

The next important event in the Baker family life occurred when Mark Baker relinquished his share of the holding of the Bow property and bought a new home near Sanbornton Bridge, a little town on the Winnepesaukee River. This town later was renamed "Tilton," in honor of Nathaniel Tilton, ancestor of Mark Baker's future son-in-law, Alexander Tilton, who operated a successful cloth mill in this thriving milltown.

Tilton offered the Baker sisters greater educational and social opportunities than were obtainable at Bow. The town's several schools included a private school conducted by Professor Dyer H. Sanborn, as well as Sanbornton Academy, an incorporated institution. Mary attended the academy and later finished a course of studies under Professor Sanborn.

It is interesting to note here what Mary had to say in respect to her education when, in 1903, she replied to the *Boston Journal* in regard to a misstatement it had made:

> I was early a pupil of Miss Sarah H. Bodwell, the principal of Sanbornton Academy, New Hampshire, and finished my course of studies under Professor Dyer H. Sanborn, author of *Sanborn's Grammar*. Among my early studies were Comstock's *Natural Philosophy*, Chemistry, Blair's *Rhetoric*, Whately's *Logic*, Watts' *On the Mind and Moral Science*.
>
> (*Miscellaneous Writings*, p. 304)

Mary's mother and father united with the Congregational Church. Its pastor, Rev. Enoch Corser, was a frequent and honored visitor at their home. He was a cultured man and grew to regard Mary with high esteem. In due time, he received her into communion and she remained a member of his church for many years and taught Sunday School there.

Here is what Sibyl Wilbur says of the friendship between Mary and her pastor:

> This pastor regarded Mary as his special pupil and the brightest he ever had.
>
> An intellectual comradeship grew up between Mary and her pastor, who, as his son declared, preferred to talk with her to any one of his acquaintance. They discussed subjects too deep to be attractive to other members of the family, which the family freely and good-humoredly admitted. Walking up and down in the garden, this fine, old-school clergyman and the young poetess, as she was coming to be called, threshed out the old philosophic speculations without rancor or irritation.
>
> One can picture them of a fine summer evening, the slender girl and the old scholar, on their usual promenade in the garden. She must have declared to him something from her philosophy,—perhaps that one drop of divine love melted his eternal hells. As she looked up at her pastor, her great blue eyes poured sunshine upon him and she smiled with such radiance that he was struck dumb in the midst of his defense of Hades.
>
> (*The Life of Mary Baker Eddy* by Sibyl Wilbur)

There is a striking contrast between this experience and the unhappy one Mary had had with the pastor of the Bow church. Now, at last, she could discuss her theological concepts with someone who was intellectually capable of understanding them. It was possible for the girl and the pastor to exchange views freely, without effort on either side to force acceptance on the other. Here were two intellectual people seeking a common understanding. Under such circumstances Mary could be most happy. Instead of feeling suppressed as she must have felt during her examination at Bow, she radiated the best that was in her.

Those talks were beneficial for her. An intellectual person feels at ease while in the presence of other intellectual persons. An unconscious contentment pervades the mind; an "at home-ness" lingers near the heart; self-confidence reigns, making possible clarity of expression; harmony is at work among God's children who are unified in His cause. Experience repeatedly shows that elucidation of one's thoughts is most effectively achieved by a free exchange of ideas and that one's point of view progressively broadens under such beneficial exercise.

In this picture given by Sibyl Wilbur we see an unfettered Mary. No longer was she restrained by another's narrowness of mind; no longer did she tearfully have to justify her theology. An "open sesame" had magically unveiled her full beauty of thought.

The Rev. Enoch Corser's son Bartlett was at this time a suitor for Abigail's hand and frequently visited the Baker home. He was to be disappointed, for he was rejected by Mary's sister, who later married Alexander Tilton. Bartlett was a cultured young man of literary tastes who had been tutored by his father in preparation for college. He never married but lived the life of a country gentleman with his two maiden sisters. When speaking of Mary in later years, Bartlett recalled his father as having said: "Bright, good, and pure, aye brilliant! I never before had a pupil with such depth and independence of thought. She has some great future, mark that. She is an intellectual and spiritual genius."

Such a eulogy, uttered by one who had spent much time tutoring Mary, cannot pass unnoticed. His statement could not have been merely a passing remark. It was, most certainly, born of repeated evidence during the many hours devoted to Mary's education. He was a highly educated theologian, accustomed to being with people of all sorts, and to helping them in their spiritual problems. Possessing such a kindly nature, he naturally would endeavor to understand the minds of those he sought to help, feeling that in this way he could do them the most good. This experience must have enabled him to acquire readily a keen understanding of those with whom he associated. Therefore, he was able to appraise Mary's qualities without any apparent doubt.

She has some great future, mark that. This was a prophecy uttered with emphasis: *mark that.* Her pastor unequivocally placed himself on record. He was sure of what he was saying; there could be no doubt in his mind as to Mary's "great future."

Prophecies uttered in earnestness, sincerity and faith, frequently come to pass; this is well illustrated by events narrated in the Scriptures. The life of Jesus affords an outstanding example. Let us briefly review how prophecies were faithfully fulfilled in the important circumstances of His life.

The world was given to understand, many years in advance of His arrival, that the Messiah would arrive and that it would be in the person of Jesus that this prophecy would be fulfilled. The evidence as to ancestral descent is strong. The purpose of God and prophecy required that the Messiah be descended through certain persons especially designated in the Old Testament. The Evangelists and apostles furnished testimony that Jesus of Nazareth was thus descended.

There was to be one circumstance associated with His birth which would point Him out in distinction from all others. He was to be born of a virgin. The world knows how true to prediction this was. Not only was there the testimony of Mary and Joseph, of the visitation of the angel and miraculous conception and birth of Jesus, but also of Mary's cousin Elizabeth, wife of Zacharias, who became mother of John the Baptist. It is known, too, that the nativity of the Messiah is also true to the prophecy given by the Prophet Micah.

We cannot help but admire the overruling providence of God. Joseph and Mary, since their marriage, had been living at Nazareth. It was in this town that they had seen extraordinary visions. They had no intimation that the birthplace of the predicted child was to be in Bethlehem; nor did they suppose that it would vitiate His claims to the Messiahship if the birth occurred at Nazareth. Probably the prophecy of Micah had escaped their notice. No ordinary circumstances would have taken them to Bethlehem; the distance was considerable and Mary's condition unsuited to the fatigues of travel.

But He who had ordained the end had also ordained the means. Emperor Caesar Augustus, ignorant of the prophecy and of the Messiah, holding the Jews in contempt, and not believing their sacred writings, was unwittingly made to fulfill the prophecy. He issued a decree to the effect "that all the world should be taxed." It became necessary for each Jew to report to his own tribe and town, unexpectedly compelling Joseph and Mary to leave Nazareth for Bethlehem (City of David), just at the time when Mary was about to be delivered of her son. Even the time when Jesus was to make his appearance had been prophesied by Daniel.

Not only has it been shown that the Messiah's coming on earth was prophesied, His ancestry prophesied, His birthplace and manner and time of His birth prophesied, but, in addition, all other important events, including His death and the manner in which it occurred, were prophesied.

Many other important instances in history can be found wherein prophecies seriously and forcibly uttered eventually were fulfilled. In Mary Baker's case there was no reason to believe that the prophecy of that venerable man, Enoch Corser, had it been known at the time by members of the family, would have been given the weight it should properly have had. The premonition of Mrs. Baker prior to Mary's birth, causing her to feel sinful because she possessed a strong conviction that the child (yet unborn) was holy and consecrated and set apart for wonderful achievements, does not seem to have been taken seriously nor to have provided a better understanding of Mary's ways. Although Mrs. Baker's intuitive conviction was known to the members of the family, there is no evidence of their having realized its real meaning. Had they done so, they would have understood that what they were regarding as Mary's peculiarities were really the formative stages of a future greatness.

Nor is there evidence that Mary was taken seriously when she declared, in her childhood, that she would write a book. Her declaration was made in all seriousness; it was a prophecy, but one without recognition at the time. Even when she confided to Albert that she must study in order to be wise, so that she could fulfill her ambition to write a book, the import of the declaration, in its fullest meaning, did not register with members of the family.

It is interesting to note a statement on the subject of prophecy by that devout early Christian philosopher, St. Justin Martyr, in his First Apology to the Roman Emperor Antoninus Pius:

> Our Master Jesus Christ, from Whom we take the name of Christians, the Son and Apostle of that God who is the Supreme Lord and Maker of the universe, has foretold our sufferings; which to us is a manifest confirmation of the truth of all His doctrines, because we see these things fulfilled according to His prediction; for this or nothing is the work of God, to declare a thing shall come to be, long before it is in being, and then to bring about that thing to pass according to the same declaration.

For people to attach but little importance to prophecies is not unusual. In fact, the opposite stand is rare. Prophecies may not be noticed until fulfillment has taken place. In Mary's case, the signs pointing to her future greatness were unseen except to her pastor. It is fortunate that there is a record of his prophecy, which was so emphatically given. No doubt he had learned of her mother's premonition and had given some weight to it when recognizing the superiority of Mary's mind. For the child had given full evidence of her unusual personality in her studies with him.

Yes, the Rev. Enoch Corser was sincere when he made the prophecy of Mary's future greatness. He had sometime before told her "Mary, your poetry goes beyond my theology. Why should I preach to you!" It almost seemed as though the good man had grown to realize that Mary was his equal in theology. And perhaps deep down in his heart he gleaned a better understanding of God's ways in consequence of his association with his pupil.

In the autumn of 1841, Mary received a severe blow in the death of her brother Albert. Albert was a likeable and intellectual young man who had made a promising career for himself. A partner in the law firm of Senator Pierce, he was a candidate for Congress when he died.

Like Mary, Albert had always suffered periods of ill health, which became progressively worse as he grew older. Brother and sister were concerned over each other's health; it was a frequent subject in their correspondence. The bond of sympathy between the two was very strong, as was shown by the incidents during his college days, already mentioned. There is no doubt that Mary had benefitted through her brother's high order of intellect, for through him her education had been enlarged beyond the scope of her other home studies. This broadening influence must have been invaluable in her future contacts with worldly affairs.

At the same time, Albert must have been benefitted from Mary's qualities, although she was eleven years his junior. For anyone sympathetically associated with Mary could not help but absorb the good she radiated. The unity of understanding between them mutually stimulated their intellectual growth. It can readily be understood what a great void must have entered Mary's life at the loss of one she loved dearly, who had been a real mentor to her for many years.

A spiritual loneliness became hers, but she knew where to turn for comfort in her sorrow. Her understanding faith in the all-goodness of God gave her the fortitude to carry on.

CHAPTER

3

IN 1837, WHEN MARY was sixteen years of age, her sister Abigail married Alexander Tilton. Mary's brother Samuel came from Boston to be present at the ceremony, accompanied by his young brother-in-law, George Glover. After the ceremony, Glover, instead of returning to Boston, departed for Charleston, South Carolina, where he intended to launch himself in the contracting business under his own name. Through vigor, enterprise and executive ability, he became quite successful in his contracting business and accumulated a considerable amount of property, including some Negro slaves. Some of these, no doubt, were acquired as part payment for his work or in other business transactions.

Not until he felt assured of a successful career did George Glover return to Tilton in December 1843, to claim Mary's hand. Many guests were at the wedding party. Concord was liberally represented and some guests came from Boston. Many Tilton friends and the whole Baker family were there, but a depressing void lay in the breasts of the Bakers, through the absence by death of a cherished son and brother.

Mark Baker could well be proud of his beautiful young daughter when he escorted her down the stairs to give her in marriage. Harmony now prevailed between them. The child who had caused him so much concern because of her religious ideas was now, through the understanding help of Dr. Enoch Corser, a member of his church and was being married under its rules. It must have seemed to Mary's father that the victory was his. He could not foresee that the spirit of love inherent in his daughter would later come into full flower and that his own stern religious dogma would be rejected.

The bride must have been happy in having the pastor she regarded with so much respect and affection perform her wedding ceremony. Similarly it must have been a happy moment for this noble church leader. The prophecy *She has some great future, mark me!* must have lingered in his memory. And he must have been conscious that he had become a better man and closer to God in consequence of working with his pupil.

Knowing Mary as we have learned to know her in these pages, we are sure that she too, on this occasion, was thrilled with spiritual emotion and memories of the help she had received from her pastor, whose patience and sympathetic understanding had done so much to lessen the tension attending her religious training. She could not help but be conscious of the opportunity given through him during recent years for the many happy hours she had devoted to teaching children in their Sunday School classes, a work she loved to perform. To her it was a privilege to teach those young ones all about God's love, the message she was decreed to convey!

Further, she had gained a peace of mind which had enabled her to enjoy writing poetry and articles for publication. Thus grateful sentiments filled her heart.

Mrs. Baker's feelings at the wedding of her daughter must have been mixed. It was not possible to share the full pleasure of her guests because the child she loved so dearly would no longer grace the Baker home. At mealtimes there would be an empty place at the table. No longer would she listen to Mary's cheery voice, or discuss subjects of mutual interest.

The loss of Albert had been a hard blow for Mrs. Baker to bear. Now there was to be another blow—the child she so dearly loved was to depart to the distant south and would no longer receive her mother's tender care. Other of her children had married, left home and done well, but of all her children Mary had needed her mother's care the most. She was the baby of the family, always frail and of a highly sensitive spirit. Her keen intellect and religious leanings had created unusual problems needing the watchful guidance that a true, loving and understanding mother alone could give. Mrs. Baker realized that her own mind and that of her daughter coincided to a considerable degree; that there was a mutual understanding between the two which forged a sympathetic bond never to be broken.

Mary too felt this impending separation keenly. She was leaving her cherished mother, who had always been on hand with sympathy and guidance. Among the host of memories that passed through Mary's mind must have been the recollection of her mother telling her, when she was still a child, that if she heard "the voice" calling her to answer as Samuel had: "Speak, Lord, for thy servant heareth."

For mother and daughter to travel along separate paths was saddening to both. But Mary's childhood was over. She was now a young woman with a superior mind and with a mission in the world. She was ready to assume responsibilities, whatever they should turn out to be, and to carry her message into new environments. She would devote her best efforts to the one she loved and would provide a happy home for him. There were many things she could do to contribute to his over-all success, for she would lean on God to guide her in such duties.

Mary and George bade farewell to their families and friends, took the stage coach to Boston and, a few days later, sailed for Charleston, South Carolina. Before they had traveled far the ship ran into dangerously stormy weather. Mary and her husband both knelt in prayer and the storm soon abated, to the surprise of the captain, who felt that a miracle had taken place.

There was between them a unity of understanding, for the young man had long ago been inspired by Mary's saintly character and had been won over to her faith in prayer. But the happy and constructive life partnership the young couple were looking forward to was not to be theirs. The story, giving the bare facts of its ending, is best told by Mrs. Eddy in *Restrospection and Introspection* (pp. 19-20). It is quoted here.

In 1843 I was united to my first husband, Colonel George Washington Glover of Charleston, South Carolina, the ceremony taking place under the paternal roof in Tilton.

After parting with the dear home circle I went with him to the South; but he was spared to me for only one brief year. He was in Wilmington, North Carolina, on business, when the yellow-fever raged in that city, and was suddenly attacked by this insidious disease, which in his case proved fatal.

My husband was a freemason, being a member in Saint Andrew's Lodge, Number 10, and of Union Chapter, Number 3, of Royal Arch Masons. He was highly esteemed and sincerely lamented by a large circle of friends and acquaintances, whose kindness and sympathy helped to support me in this terrible bereavement. A month later I returned to New Hampshire, where, at the end of four months, my babe was born.

Colonel Glover's tender devotion to his young bride was remarked by all observers. With his parting breath he gave pathetic directions to his brother masons about accompanying her on her sad journey to the North. Here it is but justice to record, they performed their obligations most faithfully.

After returning to the paternal roof I lost all my husband's property, except what money I had brought with me; and remained with my parents until after my mother's decease.

In this brief outline, the loving thoughtfulness of George Glover is clearly brought out. Knowing he could not live, he gave careful instructions to his brother masons for the proper care of his beloved wife.

Tribute is given to his brother masons for having faithfully carried out their obligations. However, there is no mention of how the young wife must have prayed in her anxiety to save her husband and how fervently she prayed for his soul when he passed to his Creator.

The brief year of their married life had been a busy and

constructive one. There had been reason for great concern on the part of Mrs. Glover because of her tender consideration of all of God's creatures and children. Before her marriage, she had formed definite opinions on the subject of slavery, a common topic in the North and in her home. Her heart was filled with sympathy for those helpless people held in bondage against their will. Therefore, upon making her home in Charleston, where slavery was looked upon as the white man's good fortune, the iniquity and inhumanity of this practice rudely came to her notice, for she found herself, through her husband, taking part in and benefitting by this heinous custom.

It must have been a sorry blow to her sensitive nature! George Glover was in sympathy with his wife's views, but the success of his business required that he recognize the customs of the South, of whose economy slavery was the backbone. Slaves were frequently given in full or part payment in transactions of various kinds, including contractual work such as George Glover was carrying on in his building construction business. The acceptance of slaves in part payment of a deal was frequently unavoidable. Thus, a contractor might find himself with a great many slaves. The kind of treatment he gave them depended upon his conscience and his means. The slaves were not consulted as to their care, of course, and suffered many cruelties, such as the separation of members of families.

It can readily be understood with what concern Mrs. Glover witnessed such inhumanities. While it was not practicable for her husband suddenly to abandon the practice of exchanging slaves in his business transactions, nevertheless he was anxious to do all that was possible to lessen this evil practice. Meanwhile, Mrs. Glover lost no time in doing what she could to help the abolition of slavery by writing articles to that end for publication in Southern newspapers. Her articles were not kindly received and editorials appeared severely condemning the author. However, every nail driven home by Mrs. Glover contributed to the abolition movement and her efforts, therefore, were of some practical value. But there remained much to be done. Years would elapse before humanity prevailed, bloody conflict would intervene and the Great Emancipator, Abraham Lincoln, would rise to the occasion and earnestly pursue his duty to humanity with a sympathetic heart.

In later years, when speaking of her bereavement, Mrs. Glover mentions that after returning home she lost all of her husband's property. Actually, much of this loss had been voluntary, because she had freed her husband's slaves, who had become her property by inheritance after Mr. Glover's death.

There was no boasting on Mrs. Glover's part for having done a worthy deed. It was natural for her to treat God's children with all the love in her heart and to free them from bondage when it was within her power to do so. The message in her heart was evolving into human expression. On this subject, many years later, she wrote in *Science and Health*, pp. 225-226:

> Men and women of all climes and races are still in bondage to material sense, ignorant how to obtain their freedom. The rights of man were vindicated in a single section and on the lowest plane of human life, when African slavery was abolished in our land. That was only prophetic of further steps toward the banishment of a world-wide slavery, found on higher planes of existence and under more subtle and depraving forms.

CHAPTER

4

THE CIRCUMSTANCES of Mary Glover's return to her old home were very different from those at the time of her departure, a little over a year before. Instead of a gay and hopeful bride, she was now a saddened and expectant mother, dependent upon her parents for support. Although she was heartily welcomed by them, there must have been a feeling in her heart that she was no longer independent and free in shaping her own life for God's work.

Mary Glover could not foresee her future. There was a child to come into the world who would need a mother's care. In the interim, she could be helpful to her mother and pursue her studies in theology. The loneliness which shrouded her did much to further weaken her already frail constitution. When her son was born, her life was despaired of and her strength was insufficient to nurse her child. Therefore it became necessary to take him to the home of Amos Morrison, whose wife had given birth to twins and who had lost one of them, leaving her with a little baby girl named Aserath. There Mary Glover's son was welcome and received good care. He was named George after his father and developed into a robust child.

Inability to care personally for her child brought added distress to one who, not long before, had lost a loving husband. She longed to recover from her feebleness and leaned on the Lord for help. There was a long uneasy road before her, one which would severely try her mettle, yet would serve to prepare her for the great mission of love which was hers to perform.

As Mary gradually grew stronger, she was able to have her little son with her more frequently and to devote some attention to writing for publication. Also, on occasions, she was able to serve as substitute teacher in the New Hampshire Conference Seminary. The spinal weakness which she had had for so many years troubled her severely at times, hindering her in performing the duties of her new life. During these intervals, it was necessary for George to be returned to his faithful nurse, Mohala Sanborn. In spite of her handicaps, however, Mary remained cheerful and did what she could to make the home pleasant for her parents and their guests.

About this time Mark Baker, who was prospering, felt that he should provide a more conveniently located home for his family, and he built one in the town of Tilton, next door to the home of his daughter, Abigail Tilton. The new house offered advantages. It was easily reached by many of the Bakers' friends, it was commodious and provided ample facilities for social gatherings.

Included among the visitors at the new home were several young men who were attracted to the young widow. One of these succeeded in winning a place in her affections. He was a young lawyer, John M. Bartlett, who had graduated from Harvard Law School and had gone to California to practice law. He and Mary had known each other for several years. A genuine affection developed between them and they became engaged to be married.

Mary's new happiness was marred by her mother's failing health. The spiritual bond between the two had tightened with advancing years, and now Mary could be especially helpful at this time in comforting her mother.

Mrs. Baker died in less than a year after moving into her new home. Her death was a deep loss to her family. Mary felt the loss especially keenly, for she had for so many years responded to and been comforted by her mother's divine qualities. Now, deprived of her spiritual counselor, she must lean directly on what she had absorbed from her mother and upon her own intuitive understanding of God's love.

The two hearts had long rejoiced and suffered as one; now her own was to travel a lonely path. She was overpowered with grief, but courage and faith were inherent in her and she was able to carry forward the responsibilities that became hers in the administration of the motherless household.

Shortly after her mother's death, Mary received news that John Bartlett had died in California. It would seem that poor Mary was not long to be allowed the companionship of those she loved most dearly. Her brother Albert had been close to her heart and there had existed a real understanding between them. She and her husband had been closely attached. And now following the loss of her mother, she was deprived of another who was so dear to her.

Four successive losses of such severity must have aroused questioning thoughts in the mind of one who harbored so much of God's love. What could be the meaning of all this? Did she have a clear understanding of the truths which Jesus had taught? Was love to be deprived of love? No, these loves were not lost; they still remained in her heart; they were there spiritually. It was only the material side of life which had passed away. Through many future years of struggle and meditation, the mystery of such happenings would be solved. Mrs. Eddy must have been referring to these losses when, in later years, she wrote in *Retrospection and Introspection*:

> Early had I learned that whatever is loved materially, as mere corporeal personality, is eventually lost. "For whosoever will save his life shall lose it," saith the Master. Exultant hope, if tinged with earthliness, is crushed as the moth.
>
> What is termed mortal and material existence is graphically defined by Calderon, the famous Spanish poet, who wrote—
>> "What is life? 'Tis but a madness.
>> What is life? A mere illusion,
>> Fleeting pleasure, fond delusion,
>> Short-lived joy, that ends in sadness,
>> Whose most constant substance seems
>> But the dream of other dreams."

Was it not likely that Mrs. Eddy also remembered as she penned the foregoing, how she had been deprived of the care of her child through circumstances beyond her control?

At first it must have been difficult for Mary to believe these trials to be a part of God's plan. They could not be, for God is Love; suffering would never be visited upon her by her Heavenly Father. No, there was something she did not understand. She believed in the efficacy of prayer; some of her prayers had been answered, but not all of them. There was a reason for this and she must search for its solution. Early Christians had freely healed the sick and raised the dead, as Jesus had done, but for many generations this God-sent gift had been lost. How did those prayers which had been answered differ from those which were not answered? Constant vigilance would be necessary before the truth could be unveiled. Mary was perplexed indeed, but more than ever conscious that it was her mission to deliver a message to God's children on earth, that they might learn the truth again and be healed as in the early Christian days.

Mary was to spend many lonely years in research and communion with her Creator before the text of the message would be revealed to her. There was a divine principle which as yet had to be unveiled. She must continue unfalteringly in the path that had led her thus far and be ever watchful for the word of the One who lovingly guides those who listen. As we look upon her finished work today and glance backward over her formative and creative years, it becomes obvious how necessary those years of research were.

CHAPTER

5

NOT QUITE A YEAR after the death of his wife, Mark Baker
married Mrs. Elizabeth Patterson Duncan, a well-to-do
widow whose brother was Lieutenant-Governor of the state
of New York. Mary, who had been in her parents' home five
years since the death of George Glover, now went to live
with her sister, Abigail Tilton, for three years. Much to Mary's
sorrow, her son was not welcomed in her sister's house, but
had to stay with his nurse, Mahala Sanborn, who had become
very fond of him. Miss Sanborn's marriage to Russell Cheney
of Groton made it all the more difficult for Mary to enjoy her
son's company frequently, because of the distance separating
the towns of Tilton and Groton. However, Mary was able
to visit her father and stepmother frequently and to assist
them in social affairs whenever her strength permitted her to
do so, for her sister's home was next door to her father's.

Now a new person came into Mary's life. He was Dr. Daniel
Patterson, a dentist and a relative of Mary's stepmother. He
was interested in homeopathy, which he practiced along with
his dentistry. Believing this form of medical treatment to be
better suited to the delicate Mary than harsher remedies, he
prescribed for her with what seemed to be encouraging results.

His interest in the widow grew and eventually he confided
to Abigail that he loved her sister and believed that, if she became his wife, she could be made well by the care he would
be able to give her. Mary was averse to the proposal but was
convinced by her relatives that it was in her interest to marry
Dr. Patterson. She did so and they went to the nearby town
of Franklin, where they lived for two years. Although they

had a housekeeper, Dr. Patterson did not permit his wife to have her son with her, feeling that she should wait until her health improved.

Because her husband was away most of the time, visiting patients in nearby towns, Mrs. Patterson was left much to herself in her small comfortable home. She led a retired life, pursuing her studies in the subject which was dominant in her mind. The long quiet hours she was able to devote to her studies were welcome to her. While she had lived with her father and her sister, the frequent social activities had precluded opportunities for meditation and study to a great extent. Had she remained in her sister's home, her advances toward the delivery of her message would have been appreciably slower. Thus the change in her life, although it was to prove undesirable from a marital point of view, was really one for which she could be grateful. No doubt she recognized that the limitations imposed by her present mode of living offered advantages in the pursuit of her most important objective.

After residing for two years in Franklin, the Pattersons moved to Groton in order to be near young George Glover, who was living with the Cheneys in that village. Life in the new home was much the same as it had been, because Mrs. Patterson's spinal ailment continued to aggravate her and frequently confined her to her bed. A blind girl named Myra Smith sought employment with Mary Patterson, who befriended her and engaged her as housekeeper. Myra proved to be a great help to her mistress, who in turn was lovingly kind to the handicapped girl. A dual good was being performed and the mutual understanding that grew between them produced an atmosphere of quiet rest well-suited to meditation and study.

Mary Patterson's efforts to be near her son were futile, for her husband continued to regard her as insufficiently strong to withstand the strain that a strong and active child would impose. Because of this, young George was permitted to accompany the Cheneys when they moved to Minnesota. They had grown to regard him as their own child and lavished on him parental affections. Mrs. Patterson's spirit was severely tried by this most difficult of all separations, but she was defeated in her efforts to prevent it. There is reason to believe that the boy's stepfather rather favored a wide separation.

Sometimes it is difficult to see, when we are in the midst of them, that events which run contrary to our desires have a purpose which is beyond our judgment to understand. What may appear a great wrong may actually be for greater good. Often one must suffer that many may benefit. In this we are reminded that O. B. Frothingham once wrote: "Who lives for humanity, must be content to lose himself."

It is evident that Mrs. Eddy realized this great truth in later years, for we find her saying in *Retrospection and Introspection* (p. 21):

> It is well to know, dear reader, that our material, mortal history is but the record of dreams, not of man's real existence, and the dream has no place in the Science of being. It is "as a tale that is told" and "as the shadow when it declineth." The heavenly intent of earth's shadows is to chasten the affections, to rebuke human consciousness and turn gladly from a material, false sense of life and happiness to spiritual joy and true estimate of being.

Looking backward, one can see that these difficult periods in Mary's life served as stepping stones, marking her way through virgin paths and serving as guides to goals as yet unknown.

As the years passed, Dr. Patterson, although a kindly and hearty man, was inconstant. Gradually, his friends drifted from him and his business affairs waned, to such an extent that he was unable to meet the small amount which came due on the mortgage on the Groton property, which combined a small mill building adjoining the home dwelling. Foreclosure resulted, and the Pattersons were compelled to vacate and lose all of their belongings. Mary was in a state of exhaustion and it was necessary for her sister, Abigail Tilton, to assist her with her carriage over the six miles of rough travel to the town of

Rumney, where the Pattersons were to reside temporarily with Mr. and Mrs. John Herbert. Before long they secured a small house and settled down to homemaking again.

The trip had been a rough one and special care had to be taken not to jolt the patient, who was suffering a great deal of pain. Myra Smith would not ride and loyally trudged by the carriage for the entire six miles. Abigail also walked during part of the trip.

Although she was given tender care by her blind companion, Mary's health did not improve. On the other hand, Dr. Patterson's affairs were bettered due to the increasing number of patients visiting his nearby office. During this period he traveled little, which made it possible for husband and wife to be together more frequently than at any time in the past.

But this was not to continue for long. When the Civil War broke out Dr. Patterson, who always liked to be in the midst of activities, was commissioned by the Governor to go to Washington. He left his wife alone with Myra Smith and shortly after his arrival in Washington sought to join the Army medical staff. When visiting the scene of the battle of Bull Run, he was taken prisoner by the Confederate Cavalry and lodged in Libby prison. Through intervention by relatives, Mary did everything in her power to secure her husband's release but without success. She was burdened with another anxiety when she learned that her son had run away from the Cheneys and had enlisted in the Army.

Eventually Dr. Patterson escaped from prison and, after stopping at Tilton, finally rejoined his wife while she was in Portland, Maine, consulting Dr. Phineas Quimby. His prison experiences had left Dr. Patterson in a weakened and emaciated condition.

Now he resumed his practice of dentistry and for a time gave promise of leading a regulated and conventional life. After practicing in offices of other dentists in Lynn, Massachusetts, he opened an office of his own and advertised for patients. But it was not possible for Dr. Patterson to remain stable for long. In spite of all his wife could do to aid him in overcoming his weaknesses, he was unable to resist temptation, and finally deserted his wife and best friend.

Poor Mary had suffered long from the severe handicaps which her wayward husband brought upon her. Her progress in spiritual matters particularly met with uphill going. Those who were becoming interested in Mary's teachings, naturally became confused and their confidence was shaken. Yet, Mary steadfastly stood by her husband in his trials and did everything in her power to aid him in throwing off the evil ways which were besetting him. She held fast to her purpose in aiding him until he deserted her and thus rejected her devoted efforts. Later she sought and secured a divorce, a step quite necessary to the welfare of her mission.

CHAPTER

6

MARY'S PATH HAD BEEN strewn with trials. Many of her years had been accompanied by invalidism. Her religious philosophy had estranged her from the members of her family and opposition to it came from many other quarters as well. The only sympathetic responses to her beliefs had come from her brother Albert, her mother, her husband George Glover, and the rector of the Tilton Congregational Church, the Rev. Enoch Corser.

She had lacked the physical strength necessary to bring up and care for her son. They had been completely separated and now he was to undergo the hazards of warfare. Her second husband had imposed upon her one difficulty after another, greatly hindering the work which was hers to perform. Further, poverty had become a daily problem, adding difficulties which would break the spirit of ordinary mortals.

There must certainly have been a reason for the rugged path which this valiant Christian leader had to tread before she could reach the clearing where the full text of the message she was bringing could be revealed. God communicates with man, through man, through the words spoken by man. Man must learn to speak before he speaks understandingly. He must learn to listen to the small voice within him and translate it into words or action. "He that is of God heareth God's words." (John 8:47) This path of learning is no easy one; it is accompanied by varied experiences, the meaning of which may never be directly understood. These experiences may be events of environment which, in turn, may be accompanied by contention or harmony or hardship of some sort or another. But whatever they are, they register on the mind and prepare it to respond to and unravel the complexities of thought.

The delivery of every important message or development is always preceded by circumstances that are necessary to its formation. "For whatsoever things were written aforetime were written for our learning, that we through patience and comfort of the scriptures might have hope." (Romans 15:4)

Habits of thought—there can be many combinations of them —enter into the scheme of things, molding themselves into a framework which becomes a nonmaterial structure. In turn, circumstances or events produce results that reflect the patterns that form the happenings of life. Thus, the weaving of a person's mentality is affected and the influences which subsequently impinge upon it become adulterated by preceding occurrences. A person may develop the habit of love, of truth, of a desire to serve, or of other beneficent qualities, or perhaps the opposite of those desirable attributes. In the former instance, that person is responsive to God's guidance; in the latter, ego stimulating independence is at fault. In the former, virtue cannot be shaken or confounded or nullified; humility and patience govern. In the latter, resentment, anger and self justification, are dominant. It is easy to adhere to the path offered by law and order, yet there are persons who lose tune with the Infinite and pursue paths of danger by choice.

All through Mary's childhood, love, patience, humility, an ever-constant yearning for divine guidance, an unremitting desire for self-improvement, permeated her being. Her right-thinking accompanied her through many periods of trial, with an ever-progressive preparation for the future work. The trials already referred to did their share in building their particular influences into the nonmaterial structure. The choice of right was hers. Through "thick and thin" she clung to the pure, the good, the divine. Gradually, she discerned the unreality of things in themselves, the immortality of loved ones who pass away. She discovered that the harboring of sorrow was an error of mortal mind. God, Who is Love, never gave sorrow to His children.

The light of truth was breaking through the wall of habit-thinking.

As we have seen, Mary was a good student of the Bible. St. Paul's Epistle to the Romans (15:4), already quoted, could not have escaped her notice. Throughout her trials, as she sought God's ways, she must always have been conscious that through patience, and with the comfort of the Scriptures, she might have hope.

From her mother, we learn that Mary was as gentle and sweet-tempered as an angel. This was the opinion of a saintly woman who recognized the saintly character of her child. It is fortunate that this remark was recorded in history, for it stimulates love on the part of all who have the good fortune to study Mrs. Eddy's accomplishments. She was a selfless, self-reliant child, of purity and honor and courage, always ready to choose her own path and unyielding to principles she deemed wrong. She was always master of herself and responsive to divine intuition. The events of her life registered in her memory with unfailing certainty and later served her faithfully in the unveiling of the message she was bringing to the world.

Not the least of Mary's attributes was sincerity. From early childhood through to her adult life, her sincerity stands out radiantly in a frame of selflessness. We are able to appreciate what this means all the more keenly when we note what Confucius says on the subject:

> It is sincerity which places a crown upon our lives; without it, our best actions would be valueless; the seeming virtuous, mere hypocrites; and the shining light, which dazzles us with its splendor, but a passing gleam ready to be extinguished by the slightest breath of passion . . . To be pure of mind, you must be free from self-deception—you must hate vice, as you would a disagreeable odor, and love virtue, as you would some beautiful object. There can be no self-respect without it, and this is why the superior man must be guarded in his hours of solitude.

The worthless man secretly employs his idle moments in vicious acts, and there is no limit to his wickedness. In the presence of the pure, he plays the hypocrite, and puts forward none but his good qualities; yet how does this dissembling avail him when his true character is revealed to the first scrutinizing glance?

It has been said that there is a strict watch kept over that which is pointed at by many hands, and gazed at by many eyes; it is in solitude, then, that the upright man has the greatest reason to be most guarded.

Mary spent many hours of solitude throughout her life. In her formative years invalidism imposed intervals of rest on her. These periods served well for meditation and communion, resulting in spiritual gains. It became natural for Mary voluntarily to seek moments of solitude as a means of advancement. Thus, the habit of withdrawing from outward distractions when contemplative work was desired was acquired early in her childhood and practiced throughout her life. The purity and sincerity of thought entertained during these quiet moments left their permanent print upon her heart.

It was because sincerity radiated from her very presence that she won devotion from her mother and brother Albert; it was sincerity which won the good will and admiration of Enoch Corser when she discussed with him her theological beliefs; it was sincerity which won the applause of the congregation and brought tears to their eyes when Mary replied to the pastor of the Bow church, when she was twelve years old, that she could only answer him in the words of the Psalmist: "Search me, O God, and see if there be any wicked way in me, and lead me in the way everlasting." It was through sincerity that she so patiently and for so long a time tried to help a wayward husband to shed his weaknesses; it was sincerity which held Mary fast to her understanding of God's love, when her father, whom she greatly respected, opposed her in her religious views.

Mary was free from self-deception. Unconcerned with thoughts about herself and self-protection, her thoughts always were directed in a quest for truth and in channels that would lead to aiding others in their life problems. She was immune to temptation, and possessed deep peace of mind.

Yet the self-control and renunciation which were unconsciously hers in no way deprived her of wholesome enjoyments shared with her friends. Her life was far from monotonous, for it was eventful every step of the way. Her moments of solitude were filled with creative thoughts which eventually appeared in a message to the world.

CHAPTER

7

Homeopathic remedies, sometimes not containing a particle of medicine, are known to relieve the symptoms of disease. What produces the change? It is the faith of the doctor and the patient, which reduces self-inflicted sufferings and produces a new effect upon the body.

(*Science and Health,* p. 398)

D R. PATTERSON HAD BEEN interested in homeopathy and practiced it along with his dental services. He had experimented on Mary with results which at first seemed encouraging but proved of no value. Still, these experiments were of great interest to Mary in her search for restored health. She had been familiar with homeopathy since the age of eighteen; her cousin, Dr. Morrill, had helped her when allopathic medicine had given her no relief.

She studied books on the subject of homeopathy and observed effects of this remedy upon others whenever the opportunity offered. How was it possible for medicines with such high attenuation to have curative effects upon the physical body? Experiments demonstrated that so-called homeopathic remedies, with medicine entirely omitted, could impart curative effects on patients when they believed they were taking real medicine. The degree of success depended upon the degree of faith. Mary's keen intellect discerned that the system was more metaphysical than medical.

Homeopathy was of growing interest in the vicinity at the time and was frequently the topic in publications and in the homes. Therefore, Mary's pilgrimage into that sphere was a natural one. It was timely because it drew to her notice, in an unmistakable way, that so-called remedies containing no medicinal potentialities whatsoever, could have more-or-less beneficial effects upon patients. She left nothing to hearsay but sought the true answer through her own experiments.

> The author has attenuated *Natrum muriaticum* (common table-salt) until there was not a single saline property left. The salt had "lost his savour"; and yet, with one drop of that attenuation in a goblet of water, and a teaspoonful of the water administered at intervals of three hours, she has cured a patient sinking in the last stage of typhoid fever. The highest attenuation of homeopathy and the most potent rises above matter into mind. This discovery leads to more light. From it may be learned that either human faith or the divine Mind is the healer and that there is no efficacy in a drug.
>
> (*Science and Health*, p. 153)

Mary already had experienced responses to prayer. She remembered how the fever left her and how she was restored to a normal condition of health when her mother had bade her to lean on God's love. She remembered now, when an anguished mother had brought to her home an infant with badly diseased eyes, and weepingly laid it on her knees, imploring her to ask God to cure the baby's blindness, she had looked into the baby's eyes and remembered Jesus' words: "Suffer the little children to come unto me and forbid them not"; and how her thoughts then went to God. When the child was returned to its mother its eyes had been healed.

These manifestations, together with others that have not been cited, could not be overlooked when exploring the mysteries of homeopathy. Mary had sensed the effectiveness of faith for a long time. She had learned a great deal on the subject through her studies of the Bible, and therefore was alert to scrutinize any evidences of faith associated with material practices. Homeopathy afforded a perfect laboratory for her experiments and she was able to prove to her satisfaction that mind played the important part in any healing and that there was no efficacy in a drug.

These explorations were proving invaluable to Mary's mission in life, for they aided in clarifying the understanding she was continually gaining through her studies of the Bible. They demonstrated by direct evidence that she should give close attention to the workings of faith. Every event in Mary's life effectively contributed to the ultimate delivery of the message she was carrying. Her experience with homeopathy was one of the many events which were so necessary to that end. Not the least helpful were those trying years with Dr. Patterson. Many worthwhile experiences were gathered during this period which greatly aided her later in understanding the conduct of different people and in adjusting her own course to meet effectively the problems at hand.

Particularly helpful to Mary were her experiences with Dr. Phineas Quimby of Portland, Maine, who advertised healing through mesmeric powers. Mary wondered if this person was really healing through prayer rather than by mesmerism. Her own experiences with prayer had not revealed consistent answers. At times cures had been effected and at others there had been no patent answer, yet the Scriptures distinctly taught to have faith in prayer. Surely and repeatedly did Jesus heal the sick, and so did His disciples and followers of early Christian days. Looking back, Mary wrote:

> When apparently near the confines of mortal existence, standing already within the shadow of the death-valley, I learned these truths in divine Science: that all real being is in God, the divine Mind, and that Life, Truth, and Love are all-powerful and ever-present; that the opposite of Truth—called error, sin, sickness, disease, death—is the false testimony of false material sense, of mind in matter; that this false sense evolves, in belief, a subjective state of mortal mind

which this same so-called mind names *matter,* thereby
shutting out the true sense of Spirit.

(*Science and Health,* p. 108)

All through Mary's life her faith in divine revelation was
supreme. Her intuitive faculties were keen and in moments of
repose, religious truths would appear, and be accepted as imaging
the precepts by which she chose to be governed. In reliance on
revelation, Mary was not unlike many of the great saints, or the
many great scientists and inventors who have contributed so
much to the world's material advances. Revelation is the great
aid when truth is sought and mortal reasoning fails.

There is no end of proof as to the truth of this. How startling
it was to Paul when on the Damascus road he heard the voice
of the Lord! Revelation is a mystery to many men. What can
be the medium of transfer from the spiritual world to that of
living man? The gulf between the two is immeasurable. It is far
beyond the limitations of scientific reasoning. The natural man
must give way to the spiritual man. It is only when one senses
the Christ within him that he is able to hear the voice from
above. He learns this truth only through revelation.

We see from the above quoted lines that Mary later learned
that the principle of all harmonious mind-action was God. She
had yet to know the science of this healing. Had Dr. Quimby
the answer, and, if so, could he impart it to others? Mary was
in great need of relief from her own suffering and would welcome his aid if she could secure it. Since he could not come to
her at Tilton, she would have to go to Portland.

Her sister Abigail, feeling concerned over Mary's physical
incapacity and financial distress, came to her aid. Her Rumney
household goods were transferred to Tilton and the faithful
blind girl returned home. Mary, by force of will, rose from her
bed and returned with Abigail to the latter's home. While Abigail
was anxious to help her sister, she did not feel kindly disposed
toward Mary's seeking Quimby's help. She had no confidence
in his methods and pointed out that Mary had always resisted
the doctrines of animal magnetism and professional spiritualism.

However, Mary could not be diverted from her purpose and secured the necessary financial assistance to make the trip to Portland. She felt sure that it was through the intervention of God that Quimby's patients were being successfully healed. Perhaps she might be privileged to learn the exact science for seeking God's aid and how to impart the knowledge thereof to others.

Finally, after much opposition from her sister, Mary undertook the trip. Her physical strength was low and the journey exhausting. When she reached Portland, terribly weak, she went straight to Quimby's office in the International Hotel. She found him an energetic man with a sincere, kindly expression. Twenty years before, through lectures given by a Frenchman, he had learned of the hypnotic power of mesmerism. Becoming interested, he had experimented on his friends and discovered that he was often successful in his efforts and sometimes seemingly effected cures. As his experiences broadened, he gained confidence in himself. But he was not sure as to the true reason for his success. He grew to believe that perhaps it was due to building the patient's confidence in the medium and directing the patient's thoughts away from his ailment.

Quimby's concept of why he obtained the results he did was always ill-defined. He had had little education and had built up a confused mixture of reasoning which he did not understand.

When Mary entered Quimby's office, she was prepared to secure God's help and prepared to meet a man who healed through religious understanding. Quimby sat beside her and, after a brief conversation in which he outlined the reasons for her invalidism, he went through with his usual hypnotic practice. Mary's faith in God's help grew intense and her pain disappeared.

Quimby was surprised at the suddenness and completeness of her response. When Mary returned the next day he was delighted to see her still in a full state of recovery. He attributed her healing to his mesmeric influence but when Mary told him that mesmerism or magnetism had no power to cure, he asked

her what she believed had effected it. She explained that it was
due to his knowledge of God's law and his understanding of
truth taught by Christ. This theological explanation of his
work surprised and pleased Quimby, and he was inclined to accept it, although he did not clearly understand its true meaning.
It was still hard for him to give up entirely the idea that he
healed through some mysterious force within his own mind.

He was delighted to have Mrs. Patterson's help in defining his
methods, especially when they were lifted to such a high level.
But he had never been a religious man and it was difficult for
him to grasp the meaning of Mrs. Patterson's theology. Nevertheless, her confidence in him was not shaken because of his
mistaken notion of the manner of his cures. She worked diligently to help him in reducing his theory, if he had one, to an
orderly and sound basis. She took his haphazard notes and
analyzed them. And although they exhibited an illogical and
incoherent train of thought, she labored on them and produced
manuscripts for Quimby's guidance which reflected her own
orderly interpretation of Christian healing.

In the Quimby experience can be seen another substantial
step toward the delivery of Mary's message to the world. By it
she had definitely clarified her thinking on the subjects of mesmerism, hypnotism and animal magnetism. We know she never
believed in them but she was able, in retrospect, to assert:

> Mesmerism is mortal, material illusion. Animal mag-
> netism is the voluntary or involuntary action of error in
> all its forms; it is the human antipode of divine Science.
> Science must triumph over material sense, and Truth
> over error, thus putting an end to the hypotheses in-
> volved in all false theories and practices. (*Science and
> Health*, p. 484) And: In no instance is the effect of
> animal magnetism, recently called hypnotism, other
> than the effect of illusion. Any seeming benefit derived
> from it is proportional to one's faith in esoteric magic.
> (Ibid., p. 101)

About two years later Mary returned to Portland again for the
purpose of gaining a clearer comprehension of Quimby's phi-

losophy, but her quest was unsatisfactory because he was still incapable of understanding his own practices.

The sifting of Mary's research brought to light the error attending mesmeric practices; it also convinced her that her own enlightenment was insufficient for her to possess a well thought-out philosophy of divine healing, although she was certain that God's way was the only true one. She had been healed of a long drawn-out invalidism and now found herself in a condition of fitness, buoyancy and optimism. She was no longer hampered in taking part in community affairs and was able freely to do services of love.

Good health aided greatly in accelerating progress in her spiritual research. She continued her efforts in tracing physical effects to their mental causes. As always, the Bible was her source of information and authority. In its pages she could depend upon finding the truth; it was for the reader to interpret the full meaning of its teachings. This was not always easy; many passages required repeated study.

This is certainly true with all of us. Casual reading of the Bible seldom conveys to the reader the true meaning of the messages which the Holy Book contains. Mary had discovered this long ago and realized the difficulty more fully than others, because she always insisted upon obtaining a clear understanding of the subjects she studied.

The necessity for diligent and repeated study of the Bible, in order to acquire a clear concept of its messages, must have dawned upon Mary gradually before she became awakened to the fact that many people were deprived of a clear understanding of its spiritual lessons because they did not give sufficient concentrated attention to what they read. In Mary's discernment of this, we see a definite step toward the delivery of her message. Through her struggles, when analyzing the meaning of the sacred Book, she must have realized that others could be helped if certain passages were explained by one who had gained the key to their meaning. Looking back now on these constructive days, it can be seen how events dovetailed into a pattern which eventually led to the writing of *Science and Health with Key to the Scriptures.*

Right-thinking was Mary's great support. She disciplined her intellect through insistent adherence to exact science, no matter what the subject in hand. No work was too great to build knowledge and she relentlessly applied herself in its quest. Her application to her tasks might well be likened to those performed by Monsieur and Madame Curie when, by their own labors exerted in an inadequately provided laboratory, they processed ton upon ton of ore to obtain milligrams of radium. The Curies' labor was great and their reward most precious. Mary's labor was unending and the reward to mankind beyond measure.

Her ability to concentrate came to her through long hours of solitude during which thoughts were arranged in orderly sequence and meanings evolved which conformed to scientific law. Her conclusions were flawless and could withstand the scrutiny of exacting minds. She was not concerned with thoughts about herself beyond the search for truth, the findings of which would enable her to help others, for she knew that truth would ultimately conquer all evil and that its virtue should be opened to all individuals.

She had already learned from her Bible that her heart should be free of all impurities; that she should think no evil of others but see only that which was good in them. Love must dominate, always, and flow to all persons, even to those who might through error seem to be enemies. The understanding of this came naturally to Mary because qualities of sincerity and love were inherently hers. Truth was her idol.

> Those who know the Truth are not equal to those who love it; nor those who love it to those who delight in it.
>
> (Confucius)

CHAPTER

8

IT WAS IN 1864 that Mary had rejoined her husband in Lynn, where he was practicing dentistry: It was not until 1882 that she was to leave there to go to live in Boston.

During her early years in Lynn, she lived in boarding houses or boarded in other nearby towns for short periods. Not until 1875 did she purchase a small house on Broad Street, thus acquiring at last a home of her own where she could carry on her work without distractions.

Before then, poverty had been a severe handicap, and it was not easy for her to secure board and lodging or quarters suitable for her theological studies. In a number of instances she earned part of her board in exchange for teaching Christian healing. She began to attract attention to her theology and to instances of healing which she occasionally performed.

With her husband, Mary had joined the Linwood Lodge of Good Templars and was frequently listed as a speaker to address the lodge, where she was regarded as a most engaging one. It was not long before she was chosen as the presiding officer of the Legion of Honor, the women's section of the society. She occasionally wrote for the press and worked on her own writings unceasingly.

When Dr. Patterson deserted Mary and thus freed her of the distractions of a wayward husband, she was able to restore the confidence of her followers, which had been steadily waning as a result of Dr. Patterson's unconventional behavior.

These twelve years were also constructive ones for Mary's mission. Wherever she was boarding, she found a way to apply herself to her writings no matter how inconvenient the surroundings. Her manuscripts became more voluminous with the passage of time. At each place she gathered new experiences, some of them unpleasant, but whatever they were, they all registered in her fertile mind and gave her an increasing understanding of the ways of her fellow men and women.

She learned how easily people's minds were influenced, for good or for bad, by circumstances of their environment; how opinions would alter from one interval to another; how even loyalty could fade and be transformed into antipathy. The sympathetic and unsympathetic, the generous and selfish, the ambitious and indifferent, the religious and irreligious—all kinds and types of people paraded before her observant scrutiny in endless procession.

With her penetrating vision and understanding of God's law, Mary easily discerned good in all these paraders. Good was inherently the possession of each one of them; and when it did not effervesce at the surface, it lay dormant within. It was true that in many cases the potential good was imprisoned by self-willed thoughts, and sometimes diluted by mental habits that were not founded upon truth. Nevertheless, because of her spiritual training, Mary could clearly see that the good was there, underneath the surface.

The fund of knowledge Mary was gathering was to prove invaluable to her gift—Christian Science. For her varied experiences made her a master in matters of organization and made possible the delivery of her message in a manner which assured not only its public acceptance but a permanent place in the theological world as well.

The writing of the message alone was a tremendous undertaking; one with endless moments devoted to divine revelation, and in transcribing that which became revealed into words the meaning of which could be conveyed to others. Of equal importance to the ultimate goal was the knowledge of people and of their ways, which Mary gained during these preparatory years.

Various events, at the time of their happenings, did not register any particular significance upon those who witnessed them. It is only as we look back upon these events, now that God's purpose, through Mary, has been fulfilled, that we see with what thoroughness He ordained His work. Fortunately, much has been recorded of this period of Mary's life, for it affords insight into the ramifications which were so essential in the preparation of the tasks that were to follow. It is unnecessary to recite the details in these pages because they are so well given in the several biographies of Mary Baker Eddy's life, especially in the admirable one by Sibyl Wilbur.

We are now able to see the purpose of Mary's affiliation with the Good Templars and its Legion of Honor. There she was able to improve her knowledge of parliamentary rules, some of which she already understood through her participation in various church affairs.

Thus, every incident in Mary's life, even one as seemingly unimportant as that just mentioned, contributed in rounding out the intellect and character of the one who was to restore Christian healing to Christianity.

It is interesting to note that while Mary was boarding with various families during her days of poverty, she often found a home with spiritualists, because they were prone to learn something of her Science. Here again were Mary's footsteps guided into channels that would be helpful to her. Spiritualism was quite popular during that era, and there were many so-called mediums who professed to be able to communicate with the spiritual world. Seances were given for the benefit of those who desired to communicate with their departed loved ones.

It is important to know that spiritualism was in no way part of Mary's theology as was later emphasized when she wrote:

> When the Science of Mind is understood, spiritualism will be found mainly erroneous, having no scientific basis nor origin, no proof nor power outside of human testimony. It is the offspring of the physical senses. There is no sensuality in Spirit. I never could believe in spiritualism.
>
> (*Science and Health*, p. 71)

Nevertheless, her relationships with those people were friendly and exchanges of thought must have resulted that were undoubtedly helpful to both. Surely her landladies could not help but gather a better understanding of Christianity and become more familiar with passages in the Bible through Mary's discourses. Her logic and certainty in her own views must have done much to convince others that the basis upon which her theology was built could not be shaken. She won respect even when her theories were not understood, and her influence for good in some instances resulted in a desire to pursue a more useful occupation. By her impelling ways, she scattered along her wandering paths germs of good that disseminated to the social make-up of the community, engendering real benefits. Although the source of those benefits was rarely recognized, Mary gained from them also. For whenever a good is done for others, reward results, though here too, its source is seldom traceable. "The more we give to others, the more we are increased" (Lao-Tze).

When living under the same roof with spiritualistic mediums, Mary was afforded opportunities of observing their various practices in communicating with the so-called spiritual world, and the behavior of those who came to attend the seances. She must have been greatly interested, because in this way she was able, by direct observation, to analyze why people were so gullible toward this popular pastime. It can readily be seen how her instinctive caution would be aroused to exercise great care in phrasing her own writings, to avoid any possible conflict of understanding which might suggest a materiality in the spiritual universe. Her views are important here:

> To be on communicable terms with Spirit, persons must be free from organic bodies; and their return to material condition, after having once left it, would be as impossible as would be the restoration to its original condition of the acorn, already absorbed into a sprout which has risen above the soil. The seed which has germinated has a new form and state of existence.
>
> (*Science and Health*, p. 74)

This illustration is thoroughly convincing—it forces the truth home with hammer blows. We can see from it that Mary had no other interest in the seances save that of enlightenment. Even more important was the opportunity to meet people, some of whom were to become her pupils subsequent to 1866.

The poverty Mary endured in those days was through choice. Her sister, Abigail Tilton, had urged her to come to Tilton to live, promising to build her a house suitable to her needs and to provide an income for its upkeep. But in making this kind offer, Abigail also insisted that her sister forego her theory of divine healing and become an obedient member of the local church.

It would have been a great loss to the world had Mary accepted her sister's offer. Revival of Christian healing would not have appeared when it did; indeed, there is no way of knowing when it would have shown its light. But of course Mary did not accept, for she could not be swerved from her path.

Her intuition told her which path she should follow, and follow it she would. Uncertainties and rough roads might lie ahead, but she knew they would fade away and that distinct guideposts would appear, which would show the direct path to follow as truly as the magnetic compass guides the mariner. Trials and tribulations might be hers, as they had been in the past, but she would continue to be patient and bear them with fortitude, in the knowledge that her errand was for the Great Master of us all. She had come a long way already. A tortuous journey might still lie ahead, but this would be safely accomplished, although incessant application to the task would be necessary.

No, she could not accept her sister's generous offer; it was not one that would benefit mankind. To accept would be selfish and that was not a part of her nature. Her life had been, and still was, bent to help others, to free them of sufferings brought on through errors of their thoughts. Were she to give up her work, humanity would be deprived of the great gift which had been ordained for her to deliver.

*

At times during this period before 1875, Mary found herself in boarding houses where she could overhear, from her room, members of the family wrangling about her views. Some were in favor of her and others against her, and bitter and undignified remarks were sometimes exchanged. Mary showed great forbearance in such situations. She realized that these were lashings which, in the service of God, one must uncomplainingly accept.

What could be their purpose? They showed, for one thing, that there could be a wide division of opinion among members of the same family on a subject considered sufficiently important to arouse anger. Was not the same true in social organizations, and even in church affairs? History pointed to frequent instances of dissension and rancor between church members. Worse, the history of the Christian religion over the centuries recited many dissensions of the most violent sort, often leading to torture and bloodshed. Had it not been so from the beginning? Had not the ministry of Jesus, the most peace-loving man who ever lived, been attended by contentions and riots?

Such thoughts as these could not have escaped one with Mary's wisdom. She knew well that any unkindnesses aimed at her should not be considered personal; that they resulted from misunderstandings of her principles, principles to which she must adhere through thick and thin. She must not resent people who did not understand. It was much better to regard them as goads for stimulating increased perseverance in the task of delivering her message. "Father forgive them; for they know not what they do." (Luke 23:34)

Mary went through other valuable experiences during her stay in boarding houses. Once when she was in Amesbury, she boarded with a spiritualist known as Mother Webster, a kindly person who took good care of her guests. Mrs. Webster liked Mary and became much interested in the latter's theories. Many points of view were exchanged. This led to Mrs. Webster's giving Mary the use of her seance room as a study.

Harmony prevailed until Mrs. Webster's son-in-law William Ellis, a widower from New York, arrived in Amesbury with his three children to spend the summer with Mrs. Webster. Ellis was a stern and ruthless man, accustomed to having his way. He insisted that Mary vacate the house, much to the objections and pleadings of the kindly Mrs. Webster. Mary decided to offer no opposition to one so ruthless. She would leave immediately, although she did not know where to go. Taking her baggage, she left the house and waited quietly on the front porch for an answer to her prayer. A violent thunderstorm was raging but that had made no difference to the brutal Ellis.

The front door was protected by a porch roof which afforded some shelter from the pouring rain. There Mary sat and reflected on the situation. Naturally, she would seek divine guidance when she felt helpless. She was calm and self-possessed for she knew that out of the unknown some sort of solution to her critical situation would appear. All she needed to do was to lean on God, as she had done so many times in the past. She was confident and would quietly remain where she found herself until rescue appeared.

These were moments for constructive thinking. Had her own thoughts been the means of creating the present inharmonious situation? Should Ellis be condemned for his seemingly unreasonable actions, or was he a sort of Judas whose evil was lent that the Scriptures might be fulfilled? Answers to such questions were not clear. Mary had progressively grown to realize that adverse conditions could not be reconciled to truth.

> Erring human mind-forces can work only evil under whatever name or pretence they are employed; for Spirit and matter, good and evil, light and darkness, cannot mingle.
>
> (*Science and Health*, p. 186)

Error of mortal mind definitely had been present. This must be expelled and the vacancy that was left filled with divine principle and love. No, Mary could not condemn Ellis, for she remembered what she had learned so well in her Bible: "Judge not, and ye shall not be judged; condemn not, and ye shall not be condemned" (Luke 6:37), and "Judge not according to appearance, but judge righteous judgment." (John 7:24).

There was no other guide for Mary to follow; it was the one she had learned to rely on from childhood. There was no bitterness in her heart, which was filled with gratefulness for all the kindnesses that Mrs. Webster had showered upon her. She was grateful for the shelter under the porch roof that was hers, and grateful in the knowledge that her appeal to God would be heard.

The answer to Mary's prayer came in a most unexpected way. She heard the door behind her being opened and two people she knew walked out—a Mrs. Richardson and a young man named Dick Kennedy. They had been fellow boarders with Mary at Mrs. Webster's and a real friendship had developed among them. Mary soon learned why they had joined her out here. If she was not to remain, they would go too. Mrs. Richardson knew of a single woman named Sarah Bagley who lived not far away and who would take them in. Accordingly, they set out on their short journey and Dick Kennedy transferred their baggage to the new quarters. They were not disappointed, for Miss Bagley received them hospitably and proved to be a person of refinement living in refined surroundings. As was the case with so many in those days, Miss Bagley was interested in spiritualism. It seems odd that Mary so frequently found herself in the society of those who followed practices so contrary to her own beliefs.

Mary's residence with Miss Bagley was quite congenial, for she found in her one who was interested in her teachings. Thus, Mary was able to promote new avenues of thought in one whose secluded life had led to rather circumscribed thinking. It was no doubt because of Miss Bagley's loneliness that she had become interested in spiritualism as a pastime. With Mary's brilliant mind and constructive temperament, her landlady could not help but gain a new outlook on life.

Young Dick Kennedy, who had gone elsewhere to board, was a frequent visitor at the classes Mary had started, for he, like others, had become deeply interested in her theories. He had a little business of his own in Amesbury where he manufactured boxes, but his interest in Mary's theology was keen enough for him to devote some of his time to these studies.

The incidents just related are illustrative of how Mary was guided along the paths leading to a definite destination, and how she always responded to the voice within her. Only one with a supreme faith could have waited so calmly and serenely on a front door stoop on a stormy night, not knowing where she could lay her head. Here was a saintly character indeed.

Events had dovetailed with great efficiency. Sufficient good work had been accomplished at the Websters; the time had arrived to leave there; work was awaiting to be done at Miss Bagley's; Mrs. Richardson was led to decide that she too would leave the Webster home; the existence of Miss Bagley and her gracious qualities were known by Mrs. Richardson; the transfer was made, Miss Bagley being graciously willing and in a position to accept the newcomers; Dick Kennedy also decided to leave, and in him was provided the helpful means of transferring the baggage. And, not least, we see in the arrogant Mr. Ellis the catalyst who spontaneously precipitated the change.

*

An event which has been considered a turning point in Mary's life occurred in 1866. When walking with some friends to a meeting of the Good Templars, she had a serious fall. The February 3rd morning edition of the newspaper gave the following account of the accident:

> Mrs. Mary Patterson of Swampscott fell upon the ice near the corner of Market and Oxford Streets on Thursday evening and was severely injured. She was taken up in an insensible condition and carried into the residence of S. M. Bubier, Esq., nearby, where she was kindly cared for during the night. Dr. Cushing, who was called, found her injuries to be internal and of a severe nature, inducing spasms and internal suffering. She was removed to her home in Swampscott yesterday afternoon, though in a very critical condition.

Mary's life was despaired of. But she refused to take the medicine which her physician prescribed. She preferred to rely upon God, and lifted her heart to Him. In *Retrospection and Introspection* she writes:

My immediate recovery from the effects of an injury caused by an accident, that neither medicine nor surgery could reach, was the falling apple that led me to the discovery how to be well myself, and how to make others so.

Even to the homeopathic physician who attended me and rejoiced in my recovery, I could not then explain the *modus* of my relief. I could only assure him that the divine Spirit had wrought the miracle—a miracle which later I found to be in perfect scientific accord with divine law.

I then withdrew from society about three years,—to ponder my mission, to search the Scriptures, to find the Science of Mind that should take the things of God and show them to the creature, and reveal the great curative Principle—Deity.

This event, like all in Mary's life, was one of a succession of events, no single one of which could be given unique credit for leading to the discovery of Christian Science. Each contributed something and had value in its particular place in the sequence of affairs. As the journey progressed and the unfolding of the objective approached maturity, so it became easier to understand the significance of the experiences being witnessed.

The incident of Mary's fall, which injured her so severely, naturally attracted attention. Although her life had been in jeopardy, her recovery had been spontaneous. Mary was unable to explain the exact reason to the attending physician; but of one thing she was sure, she had enlisted the aid of the divine spirit. Already she had gained the knowledge that all "causation was mind" (*Retrospection and Introspection,* p. 24). This acquisition was a forerunner of that which followed; it was requisite to the rounding out of faith and spiritual discernment which placed all with divine Spirit and by which Mary was miraculously healed. So it is obvious that this fall, injury and recovery, while important, should be regarded only as one of many progressive steps, providing the training and experiences which were to result in disclosure and delivery of her message.

Mary did not regard her injury and its subsequent cure to be the turning point in her career. Her language on this is lucid: it "was the falling apple that led me to the discovery how to be well myself, and how to make others so." Then she tells us that she retired from society for three years for study and research. All the years of her life, since childhood, had been filled with study and experiences useful to her purpose. Upon this remarkable foundation she would, by further study, formulate a structure that could endure forever.

Only to one with the clear mind possessed by Mary could the illustration of the falling apple occur, to disclose that there was an influence at work which stimulated a realization of an ever-present divine power ready to respond to one's call, if only one knew how to call aright. Mary felt the urge to seek this truth; she knew it could be found only by further intense study. She must do as the famous scientist Sir Isaac Newton did when he observed the apple fall from the tree—he pondered the reason for this peculiar phenomenon.

Mary too was to ponder the reason for the phenomenon which was demonstrated in her recovery, but she was to do so with a greater ultimate reward than was attained by Sir Isaac. He reasoned that the apple had fallen because of the earth's attractive force, which was called gravity, and with much study was able to relate to this phenomenon certain mathematical laws. But why and how it took place, he never knew. Even today, physicists are in disagreement. That great mathematician, Albert Einstein, thinks that gravity is not a force, as Newton believed, but a peculiar property of space; one which owes its effect through motion moving along a curve. The phenomenon which Mary was to fathom was no more tangible than that of gravity, yet she became successful in explaining it and making it understandable to her thousands of followers.

Mary showed great wisdom in her decision to withdraw from society for about three years to ponder her mission. She had searched the Scriptures all her life and on each occasion a new truth was revealed that had previously been overlooked.

Therefore, there must still be much more to be learned from its holy pages, if only one would devote enough time to them. Each sentence should be pondered if its purpose is to be disclosed.

Left alone after her fall, prostrate in bed, Mary turned to her Bible and the ninth chapter of Matthew caught her attention:

> And, behold, they brought to him a man sick of the palsy, lying on a bed; and Jesus seeing their faith said unto the man sick of the palsy; Son, be of good cheer; thy sins be forgiven thee.

When a passage in the Bible haphazardly came to Mary's attention, as was frequently the case when she opened its pages, she would feel that it was something that God wished her to see. Such a thought must have passed through her mind when her eyes rested on the verse just quoted. Jesus had recognized the faith of all those present, a faith so essential to the recovery of the sick one. Their faith was in Jesus, they were sure of His power to heal; His word was sufficient: "be of good cheer, thy sins be forgiven thee."

This verse came to Mary as a message from her Creator. That she had faith was certain, for she had long known that God healed His children. Many times had she been able to convey the light of truth to others and they had been restored to health. Need she be reminded of these things? Seemingly yes, for now God was doing so and using the medium which was so convincing to her. Mary was forcefully impressed. Yes, her faith was equal to that of the man with the palsy; she rose from her bed freed of all error. She had embodied faith through divine inspiration and saw in herself a perfect child of God. A false belief had been shed and replaced by one reflecting truth. "Our great Way-shower, steadfast to the end in his obedience to God's laws, demonstrated for all time and peoples the supremacy of good over evil, and the superiority of Spirit over matter." (*Retrospection and Introspection*, p. 26)

In further comment on her response to "Our great Way-shower," she also writes on page 27 of the same book:

If these notes and comments, which have never been read by any one but myself, were published, it would show that after my discovery of the absolute Science of Mind-healing, like all great truths, this spiritual Science developed itself to me until Science and Health was written. These early comments are valuable to me as waymarks of progress, which I would not have effaced.

There is no misunderstanding her here. There had been revealed to her "the absolute Science of Mind-healing."

How many of us have wondered about the functioning of the mind; what is it within us that governs our lives? All we have been permitted to glean is that life is always associated with intelligence. We are told that our bodies are composed of atoms of matter assembled into molecules of varied kinds, and that these in turn assemble into groups to form the communities of living cells of our bodies. But, when we are told these things, we become confused because the atoms and molecules of which we are composed are recognizable only as inanimate particles. Why, then, do they take on life when assembled into bions, organic structures, and not when assembled in inorganic materials and structures? Physicists have not given the answer.

Mary knew of this confusion; she also knew that life was always associated with intelligence and that intelligence found expression through divine mind. That is why she referred to her discovery as "the absolute Science of Mind-healing." She clearly made the distinction between divine mind and mortal mind in the following sentences:

Matter and mortal mind are but different strata of human belief. The grosser substratum is named matter or body; the more ethereal is called mind. This so-called mind and body is the illusion called a mortal, a mind in matter. In reality and in Science, both strata, mortal mind and mortal body, are false representatives of man.

The material so-called gases and forces are counterfeits of the spiritual forces of divine Mind, whose potency is Truth, whose attraction is Love, whose adhesion and cohesion are Life, perpetuating the eternal facts of being.

(*Science and Health*, p. 293)

The wisdom of these pronouncements is undeniable. Mary regarded matter as a belief in, or image of, mortal mind, to be used by it when expressing its will. She knew that it was inert, with no purpose or initiative, and that its existence could be expressed only through the workings of the mind; that without mind, matter could not be realized; one cannot be present without the other. She regarded mind and body as an illusion, which in reality and in Science rendered a false impression, and did not truly express the spiritual forces of the divine mind.

Our great physicists are awakening to the truth of Mrs. Eddy's teachings. They tell us that motion and space are not real existences, but are relative, and that time and space are mere properties which we ascribe to objects which in themselves are a complete illusion, combining space, time, matter in one unity, venturing the thought that the whole material universe is a creation of the mind itself.

There is nothing uncertain in Mary's views on the subject of life:

> God is divine Life, and Life is no more confined to the forms which reflect it than substance is in its shadow. If life were in mortal man or material things, it would be subject to their limitations and would end in death. Life is Mind, the creator reflected in His creations. If He dwelt within what He creates, God would not be reflected but absorbed, and the Science of being would be forever lost through mortal sense, which falsely testifies to a beginning and an end.
>
> (*Science and Health*, p. 331)

The contrary approach, however, was reflected by Thales when he said:

> Nothing is more ancient than God, for He was never created; nothing more beautiful than the world,

it is the work of this same God; nothing more active than thought, for it flies over the whole universe; nothing stronger than necessity, for all must submit to it.

As always, events in Mary's life progressively contributed to the achievement of her ultimate goal. This last experience not only served to correlate the understanding of divine healing which she had already acquired by degrees, but it strengthened her relations with her followers and with the public generally. Her accident and miraculous recovery had been given publicity and attracted attention to her teaching.

She knew that every human soul was in need of spiritual enlightenment and of spiritual comfort. So many in the world were misled by worshiping material possessions. Mary knew how elusive such things were; to her they were "counterfeits of the spiritual forces of the divine Mind."

Although she had been a close student of the Bible all her life, her awakening to the supreme truth had been slow. Even now there was more for her to learn: how to better understand God's messages when they reached her; how to be sensitive to divine guidance; how to leave oneself open to its presence, to open the door when the spirit knocked and to learn how to impart the secret of truth to others, once she had discovered it. No wonder Mary wished to withdraw from society. She craved long periods of seclusion for communion with her Creator.

Calmness of mind was one of Mary's great blessings. The knowledge of the inward presence of the Father gave her self-confidence and serenity in the midst of turmoil. She was able to understand others and the problems that beset them; their disharmonies were errors of mortal mind. Knowing this, she did not regard unfriendliness on the part of anyone as personal. At the same time, she understood that those errors should not be allowed to continue, they must be corrected. She must judge righteously and be firm in her position if she was to help others.

In order to efface error and reveal truth she must prepare herself, learn how to cope with the difficulties which may be found in her path. She knew she would face hostile forces, she had in the past. These forces must be overcome by love. Was not the universe sustained by harmony, harmony of motion, harmony of forces acting upon all bodies, harmony of thought radiating from a supreme governing power?

Many thoughts like these must have filled Mary's mind as she looked to the future. The tasks which lay ahead would be tremendous; they would tax her energies to the utmost. It would be impossible for her to handle personally all the details that would evolve as her work progressed. Others would have to be trained in her belief and enlisted to share in the great work. The aid of understanding and loyal souls would be welcome because Mary was not interested in self-glory, her main purpose being that Christian healing be restored to the world. The task would be such a large one she could not expect to do it alone, but she could show and lead the way.

That Mary was fully conscious that she had a divine message to impart to the world is evident when in referring to her accident in later years, she wrote:

> For three years after my discovery, I sought the solution of this problem of Mind-healing, searched the Scriptures and read little else, kept aloof from society, and devoted time and energies to discovering a positive rule. The search was sweet, calm, and buoyant with hope, not selfish nor depressing. I knew the Principle of all harmonious Mind-action to be God, and that cures were produced in primitive Christian healing by holy, uplifting faith; but I must know the Science of this healing, and I won my way to absolute conclusions through divine revelation, reason and demonstration. The revelation of Truth in the understanding came to me gradually and apparently through divine power. When a new spiritual idea is borne to earth, the prophetic Scripture of Isaiah is renewedly fulfilled; "Unto us a child is born. . . . and his name shall be called Wonderful."

Jesus once said of his lessons: "My doctrine is not

mine, but His that sent me. If any man will do His will, he shall know of the doctrine, whether it be of God, or whether I speak of myself" (John 7:16-17).

(Science and Health, p. 109)

Through the medium of this quotation from "John," Mary was keen to let it be known, as Jesus had done, that her doctrine was not hers but His that sent her. Here is to be seen a direct inference that Mary was sent into the world as Jesus had been. And there is much evidence to substantiate this belief. It was first disclosed when Abigail Baker told her friend Sarah Gault that she had recurring thoughts that her child, yet to be born, was "holy and consecrated and set apart for wonderful achievements." This and the many features of Mary's life form a pattern that seems so purposefully woven into a comprehensive mission that all who view it with understanding minds are compelled to acknowledge the verity thereof. In the same quotation also is to be seen the selflessness of Mrs. Eddy. She makes it plainly known that the doctrine she had to offer was not hers, but His who sent her.

Mary's spiritual insight again is to be seen in her quotation from Isaiah, "Unto us a child is born . . . and his name shall be called Wonderful." She plainly had in mind the new spiritual idea she had to present to the world and was not unconscious of her mother's words to Sarah Gault that the "new spiritual idea" was the "wonderful achievements" referred to by her mother. Isaiah's prophecy had been fulfilled before and now it was being "renewedly fulfilled."

> I knew the Principle of all harmonious Mind-action to be God, and that cures were produced in primitive Christian healing by holy, uplifting faith; but I must know the Science of this healing, and I won my way to absolute conclusions through divine revelation, reason, and demonstration.

There is much wisdom in this declaration. She "knew the Principle," it was "holy, uplifting faith" which was required in Christian healing. But to be able to invoke this trinity at will was the problem. Through "divine revelation, reason and demonstration" she was led to her goal and made certain in her understanding of the "Principle" which she was to further explore.

It is in line with what we know of Mary's character that she took no credit for the knowledge she was gathering for her mission. She always acknowledged the One who guided her.

> God had been graciously preparing me during many years for the reception of this final revelation of the absolute divine Principle of scientific healing.
>
> *(Science and Health,* p. 107)

CHAPTER

9

THE TEN YEARS FOLLOWING Mary's accident and recovery in 1866 were useful, constructive ones. She had reached the halfway mark of her life and had been guided through a series of experiences which helped to fit her for the "wonderful achievements" that were to come. Already she had healed the sick, reconciled those who had been separated through misunderstanding, brought happiness where there had been sorrow, engendered faith where there had been doubt. These served as demonstrations which were so necessary to her when exploring the "Principle of all harmonious Mind-action."

She had learned about human frailty and human strength; she had learned about the workings of society and its complexities. Self-reliance, which had always been hers, had steadily increased to its zenith. Meditation had aided in reaching a comprehension of the problems in hand. In matters of theology, divine principles became incorporated within her. God had laid His foundation for the structure which was to follow.

Mary was conscious of this and would always be true to the mission entrusted to her. Her forty-five years' experience would serve well in the tasks ahead, which would involve matters of organization involving many participants.

Mary always voiced her convictions because she did not claim them to be hers but rather that they came from a divine source. It was her mission to share them with her fellow men; that could not be done if she were silent about them. But to speak her thoughts was not enough, her audience would be too limited. She must write them down, so that they might be published for wide distribution.

She had learned how to watch for and glean the meanings of the voices within her and it was during the quiet moments of retirement that communion was the closest. She trusted herself, for she accepted the place which she knew had been ordained her by divine Providence. She had conquered self and was prepared to devote her entire being to the service of the Master, the One who had sent her. She would go forward in His work, and marshal others to the banner she was carrying.

The last months of 1866 and the several years following were difficult ones for Mary because she had to earn her way and carry on her work at the same time. As already mentioned, the smallness of her income necessitated residing in boarding houses where the charges were small, although the environment not always the best suited for meditative work and writing. Notwithstanding these handicaps, Mary was equal to her task, bravely and uncomplainingly pursuing her studies and work while supporting herself.

She enjoyed moments of comfort in her visits to a Quaker family named Phillips who lived nearby. They were refined and religious people and Mary enjoyed a spiritual companionship with them which brought moments of happiness into her earnest and hard-working existence. She particularly enjoyed being with their aged mother who had passed her ninetieth year and who bore the Christian name Mary also. The two Marys spent many pleasant moments conversing on religious subjects, intermingled with periods of meditation. These visits meant much to both, and it is certain that both Marys were strengthened by them in their understandings of the divine principle.

To one who is plodding the path alone, it becomes illuminating and refreshing to exchange thoughts with understanding hearts. No one can evaluate specifically the benefits which were contributed to Mary's life work by these meetings with the kindly Phillips family. But there can be no doubt that there were real benefits. They served as one more link in the long chain of events which were evolving into Christian Science.

At one time Mary had lived in the home of a Mr. and Mrs. George D. Clark. Among the boarders there were a Mr. and

Mrs. Hiram Crafts. Hiram Crafts was a worker in one of the Lynn shoe factories. Although his education had been comparatively slight, he was a thinker with a desire to increase his knowledge. It was not long before he was attracted to Mary's theology and sought to learn from her as much as possible. He became a steady pupil and applied himself diligently to his studies. Mary was persistent in her efforts to impart to her studious pupil as much learning as he was able to grasp. The Bible and her own manuscripts, which later were to form the basis of Christian Science, and other manuscripts prepared for the occasion, were the textbooks used in these studies, which were spread over many months.

Mary was successful in giving Crafts an understanding, to a promising extent, of the principles of Christian healing. He gave up his occupation at the factory in order to devote his entire time to Christian healing. This was a courageous move, because his field of endeavor comprised a relatively small community where the people were rather set in their religious views and in their reliance on medicine. With a wife to support, his practice would need to be a successful one.

Crafts had been a spiritualist before he met Mary, but her teachings had changed his views. He had been converted to the Bible and the truth it teaches. He became aware of Jesus' oneness with the Father, and how, through possessing spiritual strength and imparting faith, He effected wonderful cures. Hiram Crafts was taught that he, himself, had no power to heal the sick, but that "holy, uplifting faith," held by himself and imparted to those seeking help, was the power by which healings were effected. In his practice he was thoughtfully guided by his teacher who always rejoiced in his successes. There is no doubt that they were real, for the reports of those who had been healed had the effect of bringing others seeking relief, and he found himself doing much good.

Mary herself had been successful in the exercise of her theories in Mind-healing, there having been numerous astonishing examples demonstrated through her own faith. Now, at last, after many months of patient teaching, she had succeeded in showing the way to another. This had long been her aim, for her mission was a broad one and could not be carried out if she remained God's lone worker. Cures performed through her own intervention were incidental to her greater work; aside from serving as foundations for an increased understanding of the Science she was practicing, they helped in attracting attention to the virtues of Christian healing. As time went on, many people were brought to her banner and many sought, through her, the knowledge that would enable them better to serve God through service to man.

Mary's work had made a great stride forward. But there was still a long way to go. The many months of patient work with her pupil had given Mary greater experience in what was needed to impart truth to others. She prepared manuscripts specially suited for the guidance of her pupil. These had to be added to and revised as the plan of teaching was evolved.

In this manner, Mary accomplished much constructive work. What might seem time spent on an individual case was actually time given towards a much broader purpose. Uncertain steps were made certain. It is one thing to understand a subject or believe that one does, and another to be able to impart the understanding to another. This is particularly true in relation to spiritual subjects.

Thus, Crafts owed a great deal to Mary for the knowledge she had given him and she owed much to her painstaking pupil. Each advance made by the pupil was attained through plodding work on the part of the teacher and each step opened the way to another. A teaching technique was thereby commenced which was to be further refined by progressive experiences.

Mary was gratified by the good work of her pupil. Crafts was applying successfully the principles she had taught him; the sick were being healed.

Her pupil was in the limelight. Mary was content to stand in the background and encourage him when there were difficult places to be bridged. The sick were being healed; that was her mission. A beginning was being made through this first pupil, Hiram Crafts, and now the way was open to teach others.

The gospel of Christian Science would spread everlastingly. She was firm in her belief that this gift was not hers but of the One who sent her. All through her mission she remained firm in this understanding. Mary remembered, "Jesus saith unto them, My meat is to do the will of him that sent me, and to finish his work." (John 4:34)

CHAPTER

10

Now the time had arrived when Mary must leave the Crafts family. New fields always offered new experiences to be forged into a homogeneous whole. Each and every one in Mary's life fitted in its place and performed definite functions, as do electrons in atoms of matter.

Yearning for the affections of her loved ones at home, Mary returned to Tilton for a short visit. During her stay there, she effected a remarkable cure of her niece, Ellen Pilsbury, who had become critically ill of enteritis. But, as is usually the case, a prophet is not taken seriously in his own house, and Mary was no exception, although her niece's recovery was complete and afforded a convincing demonstration of her aunt's faith. Nevertheless, the family would have none of Mary's religion.

Shortly after this Mary left the Crafts and found her way to the Webster home and thence to Miss Bagley's, as related in a previous chapter. While she lived at these places she worked hard on the preparation of her manuscripts. The experience gained in teaching Hiram Crafts was used advantageously in clarifying her writings. It is interesting to note that after boarding for a period with a family named Wentworth, Mary returned to Miss Bagley, with whom she had corresponded for two years. She taught her the elements of Christian Science and, following this, Miss Bagley earned her living for twenty years as a practitioner although she had not fully grasped the true principles of Mind-healing, it not being easy for her to depart from some of her spiritualistic beliefs.

During this period, young Richard Kennedy, who had been

interested in Mary's teachings while they both boarded at the Websters, resumed his studies with Mary at Miss Bagley's house.

With two students, Mary was making excellent headway in developing the best methods of imparting her teachings to others. The many months of patient work with Hiram Crafts had laid a good foundation in this respect and now she was able to add to that work through students of different temperaments.

Her manuscript, entitled *The Science of Man,* was nearing completion. In addition, Richard Kennedy had become so sure of his belief in the truth of his teacher's theories that he was prepared to devote all of his energies to advance her work.

Mary was not sure that Richard Kennedy understood the difficulties attending such a move; that he knew that there would be repeated discouragements to overcome; that any departure from truly spiritual principles would be courting failure. Was he fully enlightened? Could he overcome temptations with all their attendant torments? Could he withstand the criticisms, the ridicule, the harsh treatment that would become his burden? Did he possess an earnestness of purpose which would overcome such handicaps? Could he patiently make his way through the obstructing maze that would beset his path? Did he really believe in the divine and enlightened love of his teacher? Did he believe in himself? These were questions which young Kennedy should answer for himself before entering the service of Christian healing.

Evidently Mary discerned that, on challenge, Richard Kennedy's faith was wholehearted. She acquiesced in his wish. He disposed of his box manufacturing business and accompanied his teacher to the city of Lynn, where the field for God's work would be larger than it could possibly be in Amesbury.

Kennedy, through his manufacturing enterprise, had acquired business experience which was to be useful in the work ahead. With his teacher's approval, he secured a place suitable for the work to be undertaken. It was a five-room apartment on the second floor of a young ladies' private school, the first floor being used for that purpose and the third floor for sleeping rooms. The appointments were refined and suited to Christian work. Mary's private quarters lent themselves well to meditation, prayer and work. A suitable sign was placed outside the door and prospective students were attracted thereby.

It was as if God had sent them, for there was no delay in appeals for help. The first pupils were workers in the shoe industry seeking enlightenment in matters spiritual. Their lives had been circumscribed by the limitations of their occupations and those who were attracted by the new sign sensed a ray of hope for something which had been missing in their lives.

Mary, desiring to devote more of her time to study and writing, advised and instructed Kennedy in giving treatment to those seeking relief. His successes were made known to others by those who had benefited by Christian healing and through this medium patients came in increasing numbers.

Although successful cures were being made through her pupil, Mary was disturbed by his methods for there was a tendency on his part to embrace some of the practices of spiritualists —laying on hands and rubbing the head. She always discouraged this practice in her pupils, but they found it difficult to forget the subject which was of such great interest to so many people in New England at that time.

Some of those patients coming for treatment became interested in the subject of Mind Science and made known their desire to learn something of the new Science. Mary would interview these people individually until their numbers became such as to severely interfere with the time she wished to devote to her writings. To overcome this difficulty, at least in part, she formed classes which made it possible to instruct her students in groups, thus leaving her some time for study and writing. These classes proved to be of importance in Mary's development because they demanded of her the necessity of clarifying in the minds of her pupils all points in her healing system.

Mary's students were made up of people of various religious denominations. There were Methodists, Episcopalians, Baptists, Unitarians, Universalists, and others, and some of these were interested in spiritualism. There were pupils who gratefully accepted that which was taught them, but there were others who

were inclined to challenge their teacher's theories and to inter-
mingle therewith precepts of their own religious creeds. The
harmony of a class was apt to be ruffled by people like these, and
where reasoning was ineffectual it became necessary that the
objectors no longer continue as members of the class.

Discussion would arise as to the differences between spiritualism or mesmerism and Mind Science. In these instances Mary
had to be firm in her insistence that she did not believe in
either of the former and to make clear that:

> The belief that material bodies return to dust,
> hereafter to rise up as spiritual bodies with material
> sensations and desires, is incorrect. Equally incorrect
> is the belief that spirit is confined in the finite material
> body, from which it is freed by death, and that, when
> it is freed from the material body, spirit retains the
> sensations belonging to that body.
>
> It is a grave mistake to suppose that matter is any
> part of the reality of intelligent existence, or that Spirit
> and matter, intelligence and nonintelligence, can
> commune together. This error Science will destroy.
> The sensual cannot be made the mouthpiece of the
> spiritual, nor can the finite become the channel of the
> infinite. There is no communication between so-called
> material existence and spiritual life which is not subject
> to death.   (*Science and Health*, p. 73)

There is much wisdom in these sentences and in those previously quoted on this subject, for it was a subject which had
puzzled thinkers for generations.

The Scottish scientist and theologian Henry Drummond, on
the other hand, endeavored to elucidate the subject when he
wrote *Natural Law in the Spiritual World*. In part, here is
what he wrote:

> If, as Pascal says, Nature is an image of grace; if
> the things that are seen are in any sense the images of
> the Unseen, there must lie in this great gulf fixed,

this most unique and startling of all natural phenomena, a meaning of peculiar moment.

Where now in the Spiritual spheres shall we meet a
companion phenomenon to this? What in the Unseen
shall be likened this deep dividing-line, or where in
human experience is another barrier which never can
be crossed?

There is such a barrier. In the dim but not inade-
quate vision of the Spiritual World presented in the
Word of God, the first thing that strikes the eye is a
great gulf fixed. The passage from the Natural World
to the Spiritual World is hermetically sealed on the
natural side. The door from inorganic to the organic
is shut, no mineral can open it; so the door from the
natural to the spiritual is shut, and no man can open
it. This world of natural men is staked off from the
Spiritual World by barriers which have never yet been
crossed from within. No organic change, no modi-
fication of environment, no mental energy, no moral
effort, no evolution of character, no progress of civiliza-
tion can endow any single human soul, with the attribute of Spiritual Life. The Spiritual World is
guarded from the world next in order beneath it by a
law of Biogenesis—except a man be born again . . .
except a man be born of water and of the Spirit, he
cannot enter the Kingdom of God.

In the foregoing quotations, the same thoughts have been
expressed by two great minds. The one, Mary Baker Eddy—the
other, Henry Drummond. The former, whose whole life had
been devoted to theology, who was an observer of human
traits and particularly responsive to intuition—revelation—
couched her thoughts in terms that were readily understood by
ordinary minds. On the other hand, Drummond, who also was
deeply religious, divided his time between religion and science.
On Sundays, he preached the Gospel, while on weekdays he
lectured on scientific subjects of a high order, involving pre-

cision of statement not readily followed by the ordinary thinker, but best suited for those who were more highly trained. Mary's mission was to deliver a message to the world necessitating its reception by large numbers of busy people. This was no easy task; she incessantly labored to simplify her language and to relate it closely to human experiences. Her classes aided her substantially in this task.

The tendency of Mary's pupils to associate mesmerism with Mind Science continued to be a source of concern to her for some time. She was unsuccessful in persuading Richard Kennedy to see the true light. The successes attending his practice of Mind Science led him to think that there was some virtue in the flourishes of mesmeric methods which he added, at least for the psychological effect they had on his patients. The same was true with Miss Bagley, and the newer students were tending the same way. Spiritualism and mesmerism had become so deeply rooted in the community that it seemed next to impossible to free the minds of students of this confusion. The manuscripts Mary wrote for her pupils were especially framed to overcome this objectionable practice. To that end she also freely distributed copies of The Science of Man which had been copyrighted. Touching on this period, she wrote later:

> Five years after taking out my first copyright, I taught the Science of Mind-healing, *alias*—Christian Science, by writing out my manuscripts for students and distributing them unsparingly. This will account for certain published and unpublished manuscripts extant, which the evil-minded would insinuate did not originate with me.
>
> (*Retrospection and Introspection*, p. 36)

Finally it became necessary for Mary to order her pupils to desist mingling mesmeric practices with Mind Science. Kennedy was unyielding and a parting of the ways became inevitable. It was essential for Mary to be firm if she was to give the world Christian Science free of spurious adulterations.

CHAPTER

11

NINE YEARS HAD ELAPSED since Mary's serious accident and her spontaneous recovery. During these tedious years much progress had been made in her writings, particularly during the last three years of that period, which were devoted to a complete statement of Christian Science. She applied herself unceasingly to this task and rarely appeared in public, but it was her custom to take daily exercise and rest by the sea, where she would silently contemplate nature and commune with God's glories.

Such periods were refreshing, inspiring and helpful for one who habitually leaned upon revelation as a guide in her labors. In the voluminous work flowing from Mary's pen, revelation was no facile medium. Without the self-discipline that she had attained, it would not have been possible to be so guided. For she had to close all outward distractions from her mind for many hours at a time, day after day. The purity of her thoughts freed her of confusion of mind, thus leaving a crystal clear window through which spiritualized thoughts would reach her.

A young man named George Clark, who was an author of stories for boys, accompanied Mary one day to see a publisher in Boston with a view to having her manuscript published, as well as his own. The publisher upon whom they called rejected Mary's book with the comment that it was a subject which offered few commercial possibilities. However, he did accept George Clark's story on sea-going life, which he felt would sell.

On the journey home, Mary rejoiced with George Clark upon his success and was in no way discouraged by the rejection of her own writings. She could readily appreciate the publisher's point of view, and graciously accepted it. It must find its way to

God's children through channels that would be opened through devotion to His purpose.

Mary had knocked at the wrong door and she realized it quickly. No harm had been done; instead she was grateful for being shown which path to follow. The publication of this important revelation must not be carelessly handled; it must not depend upon the whims of a publisher who had no understanding of the importance of the message it conveyed. She understood that the publication of the work of many years of spiritual research and divine revelation should be carefully guided by none other than the one to whom this great message was entrusted.

Mary now had a thorough understanding of how she should proceed. It would not be simple, but she would find a way of giving the book wide distribution and honored reception. The inward guide, the infallible voice was as ever with Mary; her steps could not be halted and she would not falter. She was born a true Christian; the Christian spirit was ever in her and her growth was one of ascending stages wherein that influence found freer and freer outlet as she grew in years.

This is evident in the evolution of the text that was soon to be printed! Just as it was with Mary's message, the manuscript grew by degrees as though it were a living plant, with all the marvels of structure of a growing plant and its perfection of formation.

While walking home with George Clark from the Lynn station after their visit to the Boston publisher, Mary suddenly stopped as they were passing a church. Gazing intently at it she said to Clark, "I shall have a church of my own some day."

Had this been said by an ordinary person, it could be passed over without notice, but when uttered by Mary it must be noted with all seriousness. It should not be overlooked that when Mary was a child she had made it known that she would write a book some day and that she must prepare herself for such a worthy task. While it is likely she did not, at the time, clearly visualize the nature of her desire or premonition, she must have felt the inward glow of a duty to be fulfilled when she grew up. The statement that she would write a book had now proved to be no idle prophecy. She was in full womanhood and the book had been written and was soon to be printed. Her grateful heart knew it to be the fruit of many years' communion with the Divine Guiding Spirit.

And now she was saying: *I shall have a church of my own some day.* This prophecy was given with the same clear emphasis and positive conviction as was the first.

To those who understand and respect the infallibility of prophecy when sincerely uttered by one who is sensitive to revelation, there can be no doubt as to the positiveness of Mary's statement. There could be no doubt at the time it was made that it would be fulfilled. And fulfilled in large measure it has been, and the measure is becoming ever and ever larger and is spanning the world.

It was in the spring of 1875 that Mary purchased her modest home in Lynn. There she secured the quiet atmosphere she needed for the conducting of her classes and for putting the finishing touches to her manuscript. Not until October of that year was it released by the printer. One thousand copies of the first edition were printed, many copies of which found their way into the hands of numbers of Christian Science pupils. The distribution of the remainder was slow and was not considered satisfactory, but as we look backward, the slow public response was to be expected because there would be little reason for interest in *Science and Health* for those other than students of that subject. Therefore, broadcasting Christian Science healing would not be successful at this stage. First, increasing numbers of students would have to be enrolled and wide interest aroused through resultant healings. Like all early beginnings in worthwhile things, especially new movements relating to religion, progress at first was very slow. Persistence would be necessary and experience gained along the way would dictate how best to proceed.

A great deal of work had gone into the writing of *Science and Health*, but little had been done to prepare for its public acceptance. This in itself would be a huge undertaking, requiring years of unremitting work by Mary herself. The years immediately following were to give Mary experiences which would greatly help her in mastering the manifold problems confronting her as she marched forward. The issuing of the first one thousand copies of *Science and Health* could in no way be considered as the delivery of the message with which she was entrusted. Not until it was accepted on a world-wide basis could Mary feel that her mission had been fulfilled.

Mary had other problems. There was unrest among some of her students. People do not all think alike, and when individuals enroll in a class or elect to study the same thing, it does not mean that they are all of the same mind or that they will interpret that which is taught in exactly the same light. Therefore, it was not unnatural that differences of opinion should develop among Mary's students. There were many who grasped the meaning of that which had been taught them, and who were loyal to their teacher and to the Science they had learned. But some of the less serious pupils were apt to cause disharmony. The problem of jealousy arose. Some of those who had taken on responsibilities in the advancement of the work were unable to see clearly that as progress was made it became necessary to open the way by shifting personnel.

Conflicts of this nature were not always easy for Mary to iron out, but she applied herself to the task serenely, at the same time busying herself with improvements in the text of *Science and Health* in preparation for second printing. She was not waiting for the first issue to be completely distributed but, as was her custom to do, was forging ahead. She knew that her goal could be reached only by plodding and that each step taken toward it opened the way for the next one. It was fortunate that disharmony occurred among some of the students, for this too proved to be helpful in Mary's education, serving to guide her, in her future work, against the pitfalls created by the many frailties of human nature.

CHAPTER

12

THERE CAN BE NO BETTER way to open this chapter than to quote Mrs. Eddy:

A TRUE MAN

My last marriage was with Asa Gilbert Eddy, and was a blessed and spiritual union, solemnized at Lynn, Massachusetts, by the Rev. Samuel Barrett Steward, in the year 1877. Dr. Eddy was the first student publicly to announce himself a Christian Scientist, and place these symbolic words on his office sign. He forsook all to follow in this line of light. He was the first organizer of a Christian Science Sunday School, which he superintended. He also taught a special Bible class; and he lectured so ably on Scriptural topics that clergymen of other denominations listened to him with deep interest. He was remarkably successful in Mind-healing, and untiring in his chosen work. In 1882 he passed away, with a smile of peace and love resting on his serene countenance. "Mark the perfect *man*, and behold the upright; for the end of *that* man is peace" (Psalms 37-37).

(Retrospection and Introspection, p. 42)

No higher tribute could be made than the one Mrs. Eddy quoted from the Psalms, and this tribute was justly deserved.

Mr. Eddy's work in association with Mrs. Eddy was for a brief five years only. These years were filled with Christian Science accomplishments which demanded the sort of teamwork that was possible only with a united spiritual purpose. Asa Gilbert Eddy was a man of refinement, strong in purpose, mild in disposition, keen in understanding, spiritually minded, of unblemished integrity, self-effacing and self-sacrificing, conscientious in duty, never vacillating but always guided by reason, just and tolerant, and wedded to the service of Christian Science.

Their common spiritual purpose had brought these two people together. Mary had arrived at a stage in her travels that would, for the next five years, require the aid of one who would be ever watchful of a multitude of details which could not be cared for single-handedly, and it was thus that she found greater freedom to evolve ways and means for permanently establishing Christian Science on firm foundations. Before this could take place, much organizing work would be required, which could not be undertaken until the many difficulties presently confronting her had been cleared away.

The dissensions among some of the pupils, previously mentioned, were gradually growing and had reached a state where further advances were being retarded by them. Serious trouble arose with one Daniel Spofford, whom Mrs. Eddy had made business manager in relation to the finances of the first and second editions of *Science and Health*. This work did not run smoothly, mainly because the community had not been ready to absorb all copies of the first printing. The student who filled the role of business manager became self-opinionated as to procedure and adamantly refused to respect Mrs. Eddy's directions. Instead, he left his former teacher and benefactress, and decided to go into business for himself. He did all he could to hinder the one who had so patiently educated him in the Science of Mind-healing. This situation resulted in leaving unfinished the printing of the second edition of *Science and Health*, which was at that time under way, and in leaving Mrs. Eddy without the means of completing it. Then this man joined with several other people in an effort to injure the one who not only had taught them, but who had helped them succeed in their practice, even aiding them financially in some instances. Their jealousies rose to a point where lawsuits were brought which, because of the inconsistencies of the claims, were lost, and they were left in a muddle.

During this period, Mrs. Eddy's vicissitudes were many. Each bore its own lesson, each fortified her character, each pointed in which direction she should go forward, each emphasized the desirability of omitting, whenever possible, the personal equation where God's work is involved. Only those who were selflessly interested in the great cause could be entrusted to share in a work so important.

The demand upon Mrs. Eddy was becoming so great that she could no longer attend to her writing and planning in an orderly way. Patients insisted on receiving her personal attention and wanted her to teach them the Science of Mind-healing. Mr. Eddy, who had been an apt student, soon was able to be useful in a practical way. Not only did he successfully practice Mind-healing, and thus relieve Mrs. Eddy of some of these duties, but he also relieved her of some of the business details.

It became obvious to Mrs. Eddy that past practices could no longer be suitably applied to the future growth of Christian Science. These practices had been outgrown already, as present events were demonstrating. It was no longer practical for her to conduct classes personally and give attention to all those desiring to be taught individually or in need of Christian healing. Much of this work would have to be allotted to others. Her own time then could be effectively devoted to preparing for the third edition of *Science and Health* and to setting in motion the best means for its effective circulation.

Some kind of school was becoming necessary, one through which sincere and earnest believers could be trained and sent forth to spread the message. And we should remember Mrs. Eddy's prophecy: "I will have a church of my own some day." Much preparation for this future event would be necessary. An effective church organization would first be required. It could meet in improvised or temporary quarters until it grew in experience and in members. These were the momentous undertakings which Mrs. Eddy had now to do. They were distinctly a part of her mission and she was now clearing the way for this work.

CHAPTER

13

MRS. EDDY REALIZED that the work confronting her could not be effectively carried out in the city of Lynn. It had served well enough as a training field for providing the background so essential to further progress. But its population was relatively small and was made up mostly of manufacturing workers, who had not had the advantages of education in a broad sense. Therefore, it was not easy for many of them to comprehend readily the new doctrine she had to offer. In order for her to make real headway, she needed a larger sphere, one in which the population had a broader cross section of interests and education. Accordingly, she chose Boston as offering the advantages so necessary for the more rapid advancement of her mission.

The distance between the two cities being short, little inconvenience was felt by Mrs. Eddy in her weekly visits. At first she lectured on Sunday afternoons in the Shawmut Avenue Baptist Church, and, later, in the Parker Memorial Hall on Appleton Street, which had a seating capacity of four hundred.

It was natural that her lectures should draw but few people at first, because Mrs. Eddy was not well known in Boston yet and the advance publicity had been limited. But news of the wonderful lecturer they had heard was spread by her listeners among their friends. In this way, more and more people became interested and in time the Parker Memorial Hall was filled to capacity at every gathering.

The Boston audiences were on a different cultural level from those from the Lynn factories. They showed a marked interest in the doctrine presented to them, were less inclined to shrink within themselves, and appeared to comprehend the philosophy propounded more readily. They appreciated the fact that they were being accorded a great privilege in having one so far advanced in theology lecture to them and radiated a desire to absorb more of the new Science.

Mrs. Eddy felt the responsiveness of her audiences and this did much to hearten her in her work.

When listening to her lecture, Mrs. Eddy's audiences could truly say: "What hath God wrought?" as did Samuel Breeze Morse in his first message to Congress, sent over the wire between Baltimore and Washington by his newly invented magnetic telegraph system. They had before them a woman of impressive appearance, with perfect poise, perfect diction, pleasing personality, sound reasoning with an intimate knowledge of the Bible from beginning to end; with a message which would bring infinite good to mankind.

Mrs. Eddy had learned well the lessons placed in her path as she wended her way from childhood to these first Boston days! The Sunday School classes which the youthful Mary had taught, the occasions when she had served as a substitute teacher at the New Hampshire Conference Seminary and when she had been presiding officer of the Linwood Legion of Honor, the many classes she had taught and lectures she had given in the city of Lynn—all these had served as training schools fitting her for the work she was now entering.

The responsiveness of her Boston audiences did much to hearten Mrs. Eddy in her work. And the great teacher's capacity for work was superhuman. Most people would have required a week's preparation for each Sunday's lecture. Such time could not be granted Mrs. Eddy, because there was still so much for her to do in Lynn, and she must devote herself to the many calls for service which, as yet, she alone could answer. Yet, in spite of all the demands on Mrs. Eddy's time, her Boston lectures were of a very high order. The students who were loyal to her were helpful in many ways and would become more so as her work progressed. Some of these were to become the first workers and nucleus of a progressively expanding organization which now carries the name Christian Science.

During the difficult days of transition from Lynn to Boston,

Asa Gilbert Eddy was a great comfort and help to Mrs. Eddy. Not only did he spread much good by practicing Mind-healing, but he devotedly attended to the many business details that kept arising. He was respected by all of the loyal workers and was firmly true to Mrs. Eddy's leadership, which he held to be divinely guided. His work dovetailed into that of the main structure with harmonious efficiency. During hours of relaxation, husband and wife lived in surroundings which were simple yet full of charm. They enjoyed a harmonious atmosphere of affection and esteem. These were moments of spiritual growth.

Visitors to their home were always entranced by Mrs. Eddy's radiance. Many of these visitors were notables. They sought her grace and were healed of their sufferings in a miraculous way. Many of them later showed their everlasting appreciation and gratitude by the aid they gave in the founding of Mrs. Eddy's church.

Visitors impressed with the harmony of Mrs. Eddy's home, and her calm serenity and cheerful manner, must have wondered how it was possible for her to be so self-possessed. For at that time there were quarreling students who, through personal jealousies, were misleading public opinion so that it was increasingly difficult to spread the truth. But those who had known Mrs. Eddy from childhood could readily account for her peace of mind, under conditions which would be quite disturbing to other mortals. They could remember that from infancy she had been a close student of the Bible; that she had been constantly absorbed in the spiritual lessons it contained; and that she was, body and soul, immersed in its atmosphere. She knew God was good and that He was with her at all times and always would be; His presence was charging her innermost being, giving her certainty and strength. The errors of those about her shrank into oblivion. The responsibility was not hers but rested with God; His will be done—not hers. This idea was always present in her thoughts. She could serve God best by viewing without fear the errors of His children while they were groping in darkness, for ultimately they would be led onto the right path. Briefly, she felt the Kingdom of God within her.

CHAPTER

14

M RS. EDDY'S DETERMINATION had not faded since the day she
had told George Clark: "I shall have a church of my own
some day." Of course, there were other problems to be solved first;
the Lynn classes and the Boston lectures could not be neglected.
These and other activities prevented Mrs. Eddy from undertaking the organization of a church of permanent character on a
large scale.

It is often really best that experiences from small beginnings
disclose the way to broader paths. Mrs. Eddy remembered that
only about a year before a tentative organization had been set
up by eight students who were to meet occasionally for church
services, and that this organization had failed. A repetition
of failure should be avoided. Accordingly, in 1876, an organization known as the Christian Scientist Association was formed.
It served to hold the students together for their regular work and
meetings.

This was followed by the incorporation of a church society,
and in August 1879 a charter was issued by the state proclaiming
that the Church of Christ Scientist was to be established in
Boston. At first there were twenty-six members in the new
church. Mrs. Eddy was elected president and ordained as its
pastor.

Thus, the great prophecy was fulfilled. It is interesting to
record that this church organization continued in existence until
1892, at which time it was reorganized. Its permanence shows
how well Mrs. Eddy had planned her work.

Church meetings were held in the parlors of the homes of
various members until 1880, when Hawthorne Hall on Park

Street, Boston, became the meeting place where church services were held regularly. A new atmosphere was found here, one which imparted to those present a feeling that they were assembled in God's house, gathered there to commune collectively with their Creator.

The first meeting held there must have been a happy one for Mrs. Eddy. Her dream was materialized; her gospel could now be preached to the multitudes. This was no beginning—Mrs. Eddy tells us in *Science and Health* that there are no beginnings —but it was an important stride forward, one which would serve as a marking point by which growth could be measured from then through all future years. It was the infant that, with careful nurturing, would steadily grow in stature. There would be growing pains, to be sure, but these would involve no more than the natural difficulties encountered in life. At last Christian Science would become publicly known. It had burst through its confinement of restricted gatherings. Eventually congregations would meet in all Christian cities of the world to take part in the Lesson-Sermon given in the Christian Science Sunday service.

But Mrs. Eddy's work was not yet finished. Her message had long been traveling, yet its delivery was still incomplete. Refinements in its text must be effected, church organization improved, and church services revised.

To meet the demands of the increasing number of people seeking instruction in Christian Science, Mrs. Eddy now organized the Massachusetts Metaphysical College, for which a charter from the state was obtained. Six of her students were designated as directors and also served as teachers under Mrs. Eddy's direction. As well as being president of the institute, she also taught some of its classes.

The organization of the college showed foresight on Mrs. Eddy's part, for it served to give increasing numbers of people an intimate understanding of Christian Science and this would have been impossible had she tried to do the work alone.

The pressure on Mrs. Eddy to transfer her principal activities from Lynn to Boston was becoming increasingly great. Lynn had served as an admirable proving ground, but its usefulness was outlived. And it was now time to broaden the arena of work.

There were many reasons for this. The dissensions among the disloyal and jealous pupils in Lynn showed they were no longer of value. As for those students who were true to their teacher, they would continue their spiritual growth and be helpful to her wherever she might go. Another problem was the matter of copyrighting. Mrs. Eddy realized the necessity of copyrighting her manuscripts because unscrupulous persons were appropriating passages of her text as their own. To secure legally unassailable copyrights, it would be necessary for Mrs. Eddy to be in Washington for the purpose. These circumstances, taken together, provided the urge for moving forward.

Before taking up their residence in Boston, Mr. and Mrs. Eddy went to Washington in January 1882, and remained there for about three months. They secured a comfortable apartment with a good view of the Capitol.

Mr. Eddy spent his time in Washington studying copyright law and applying the knowledge he gained to obtaining copyright security for his wife's Christian Science manuscripts.

Meanwhile, Mrs. Eddy was not one to rest idly in her new surroundings, even though they were only temporary. She was soon as busy as ever from early morning till late at night. The change of environment was refreshing and beneficial to her. Although she had never shown signs of fatigue, the move to Washington can be regarded as providentially providing a stimulating interlude in her difficult work.

Her surroundings were, indeed, stimulating to one who was so easily responsive to the good in the world. She went ahead with her work with boundless buoyancy, corresponding with her helpers in Lynn and in Boston, forming classes and giving lectures on Practical Metaphysics.

CHAPTER

15

WHILE MR. AND MRS. EDDY were still in Washington, they
had, through the aid of her students, rented a house in
Boston. It was a four-story gray stone structure located on Columbus Avenue, large enough to serve both as a residence and as a
base for the activities of the Massachusetts Metaphysical College. It was simply furnished and had the atmosphere of refinement so typical of Mrs. Eddy's tastes. Several students came to
live there and tutored in the class work. The ground was now
set for the next important lap in the long journey of God's messenger of love.

But now something happened to sadden this loving spirit
deeply. After a brief illness, Mr. Eddy quietly passed away in his
sleep in the early morning of June 3, 1882. No blow could be
more severe to Mrs. Eddy; it was as though her whole life's
purpose had been shorn of divine support. How could she continue without the kindly help and companionship of her husband. He had been a perfect husband, a perfect helpmate in
the work of God. "Mark the perfect man, and behold the upright: for the end of that man is peace." (Psalms 37:37).

His part of the work was finished. He had always been conscientious and nothing was left undone that was his to do. Difficulties had crossed his path, as they frequently do when great
events are brewing, but these were cleared away and the horizon
again shone with the radiance of an unclouded sky. There was
within him a compendium of human virtues.

Perplexity naturally arose in the minds of Christian Science
students. Here was one so closely affiliated with the subject of
their studies, who had so successfully been the means of healing

others, yet who had not healed himself. Here was one who had been in close affinity with their teacher, who had been the means of so many miraculous cures, yet he had not been saved by the one who loved him so much.

These were natural thoughts for those early Christian Scientists to entertain. But they were conscious that in the material world, the world in which they consciously lived, death denoted the ending of the mortal man but not of the spiritual man; that death accompanied the belief in material life without reflecting true spiritual life. Upon reflection, it was remembered that there was no beginning or ending in life.

> The infinite has no beginning. This word *beginning* is employed to signify *the only*—that is, the eternal verity and unity of God and man, including the universe. The creative Principle—Life, Truth and Love —is God. The universe reflects God. There is but one creator and one creation. This creation consists of the unfolding of spiritual ideas and their identities, which are embraced in the infinite Mind and forever reflected. These ideas range from the infinitesimal to infinity, and the highest ideas are sons and daughters of God.
>
> (*Science and Health*, p. 502)

Life was the one supreme intelligence—God—and God expressed Himself through man.

The early Christian Scientists remembered other things Mrs. Eddy had taught them:

> Man is immortal, and the body cannot die, because matter has no life to surrender. The human concepts named matter, death, disease, sickness, and sin are all that can be destroyed.
>
> If it is true that man lives, this fact can never change in Science to the opposite belief that man dies. Life is the law of Soul, even the law of the spirit of Truth, and Soul is never without its representative. Man's individual being can no more die nor disappear in un-

consciousness than can Soul, for both are immortal.

(Science and Health, p. 427)

Also this:

"THY WILL BE DONE!" This is the law of Truth to error. "Thou shalt surely die". This law is a divine energy. Mortals cannot prevent the fulfillment of this law; it covers all sin and its effects. God is All, and by virtue of this nature and allness He is cognizant only of Good. Like a legislative bill that governs millions of mortals whom the legislators know not, the universal law of God has no knowledge of evil, and enters unconsciously the human heart and governs it.

(Miscellaneous Writings, p. 208)

Mrs. Eddy had had a companion in the special tasks that were then to be done. She would now go forward alone and build a finished edifice.

When a loved one is lost, sorrow is not easy to quench; reason may be invoked but it in no way assuages the mental anguish. In this respect, Mrs. Eddy differed little from other deeply sympathetic souls. But she struggled heroically with the human sense of grief that had overtaken her. Her paths had led her through many grief-stricken shadows and this one weighed upon her as the darkest of all, but fortitude continued to serve her as ever in her deep need.

Her calmness of mind had not forsaken her; it never had and never would, for her heart dwelt in love, love for her departed one, love for God and love for all His children. She knew that the present darkness was but a passing shadow falling upon mortal mind; that sorrow is false and cannot live; that she could conquer herself and replace this unreal burden by its counterpart, joy, which is real and cannot die. She affirmed, "I believe in God's supremacy over error, and this gives me peace."

(Post, June 5, 1882)

Still, because of the severe mental strain which Mrs. Eddy suffered, it was thought desirable that she temporarily leave the scene of the unhappy event and seek the quiet country, where she could relax and pursue spiritual comfort and growth. This, then, was what she decided to do.

But first there was a problem she must solve. Many matters in Christian Science affairs which Mr. Eddy had taken care of must be attended to. A reorganization of these activities was necessary. Therefore, before Mrs. Eddy retired for rest in the country, she telegraphed Arthur True Buswell of Cincinnati to come to Boston for consultation. Mr. Buswell had been a student of Mrs. Eddy, and she had delegated to him the carrying on of Christian Science work in Cincinnati.

It was arranged that during Mrs. Eddy's absence, several students would carry on the work in the Columbus Avenue home. The good work must continue, even though its acceleration be temporarily impeded. Its full swing would be resumed when its leader had obtained new bearings. These she would seek through inspiration and revelation, while resting among the beauties of nature. These were bountiful in the lovely little village of Barton, Vermont, where Mr. Buswell had opened his country home for her stay.

It is easy to imagine that Mrs. Eddy's thoughts would not remain idle during her sojourn there. Grief was hard to bear, but in one with her noble senses a catalyzing agent would be at work further purifying motives which already were filled with good.

> Great grief makes sacred those upon whom its hand
> is laid. Joy may elevate, ambition glorify, but sorrow
> alone can consecrate. (Horace Greeley)

During Mrs. Eddy's stay in Barton, plans for her future organization matured in her thoughts. She mentally reviewed her students and their respective capabilities and carefully planned the roles they were to fill. Her thoroughness in such matters had not been impaired by the ordeal she had undergone, but had instead become greater through the dictates of necessity. She summoned a former pupil, Calvin A. Frye of Lawrence, Massachusetts, who joined her on her return trip to Boston. On this trip, she apprised him of her need of someone who would serve in a confidential capacity and care for some of the business details of a growing organization.

After discussing the subject with Mr. Frye, Mrs. Eddy questioned him as to his willingness to serve, and he gladly consented to do so. No mention was made at the time of the foresightedness of her late husband who, in his desire to strengthen Mrs. Eddy's organization, had several months before gone to Lawrence for the purpose of inquiring into Mr. Frye's record. The services of this faithful man, who already was well founded in the doctrine of Christian Science, commenced two months after Mr. Eddy's death and continued until Mrs. Eddy had completed her travels on this earth.

There Mrs. Eddy showed great wisdom in appointing Calvin A. Frye to this high position for he proved efficient and untiring in carrying out his many duties. His executive ability never failed him. He was a constant member of Mrs. Eddy's household, and his mild manner made all activities run with unruffled smoothness. He devotedly carried out Mrs. Eddy's wishes, knowing that they came through her from God. Fully recognizing the true meaning of her mission on earth, he considered it a privilege to serve one who was appointed by the great Master.

CHAPTER

16

SHORTLY AFTER MRS. EDDY'S return to Boston, she moved to a larger house next door, in order to provide more suitably for the growing Massachusetts Metaphysical College. A number of her practitioners made their home there, and shared the meeting rooms on an office hour basis.

Mrs. Eddy retained special rooms for her own private work. She devoted several hours a day to teaching and lecturing in the classes of the Metaphysical College, which she wholly directed. Large numbers of students were attracted to the course, aggregating four thousand in a period of eight years of the college's existence. These classes served in building a broad foundation for Christian Science. While some of the students were ill fitted to absorb the new doctrine, and contributed little or nothing to its advancement, there were a great many who became actively associated with Christian Science and cooperated in its growth. The paths of the latter radiated to points near and far, thus broadening the sphere of interest in the doctrine.

In Boston, the congregation of Mrs. Eddy's church continued to expand "and at every epoch saying, 'Hitherto hath the Lord helped us.'" (C M, 18). Those who had been healed attracted others, who were drawn to gain an increased understanding of the Bible. Mrs. Eddy's sermons were very enlightening and won the respect of all who listened with understanding and a desire for spiritual growth. There were critics, it was true, some severe and relentless, but there always are dissenters when something new is given to the world. We should be grateful to those who publicly aired their disbelief. For with such airing, their errors were precipitated to the depths of darkness, and the truths permitted to rise to the surface to illuminate the horizon so all could see and accept. Thus, what might have appeared on the surface as a threat to the new doctrine was actually most favorable to it. "Truth is truth to the end of reckoning" (Shakespeare).

With the growth of the church, the establishment of an order of procedure and rules for its service became increasingly desirable. Its leader, with her usual thoroughness, exercised her guiding hand at each "epoch" in its progress. In respect to its rules and by-laws she later wrote:

> The Rules and By-laws in the Manual of The First Church of Christ, Scientist, Boston, originated not in solemn conclave as in ancient Sanhedrin. They were not arbitrary opinions nor dictatorial demands, such as one person might impose on another. They were impelled by a power not one's own, were written at different dates, and as the occasion required. They sprang from necessity, the logic of events,—from the immediate demand for them as a help that must be supplied to maintain the dignity and defense of our Cause; hence their simple, scientific basis, and detail so requisite to demonstrate genuine Christian Science, and which will do for the race what absolute doctrines destined for future generations might not accomplish.
>
> (*Miscellaneous Writings*, p. 148)

In the last sentence, the motive of the world's great missionary may be clearly discerned.

Now that Science had been revealed, it must never again be allowed to pass into oblivion. Her task was not only to deliver God's message to the human race, but to establish its precepts so firmly that they would never again be lost.

Some might call the unseen power impelling Mrs. Eddy forward the result of lofty dreams, rather than the revelation to which she declared herself indebted. It has already been noted that throughout her whole life she maintained herself responsive to divine guidance.

CHAPTER

17

As PUBLIC INTEREST in Christian Science grew, the demand upon Mrs. Eddy's time and her writings increased. She worked unceasingly—healing, teaching, interviewing, lecturing, and delivering her Sunday sermons. To a certain extent she was aided by those of her students who became active workers, but this help was not sufficient to meet the needs of her increasing number of followers. Many who became healed of error were awakened by a desire to learn and to serve the great cause.

For some time, Mrs. Eddy had been conscious of the need for a publication through which those interested in Christian Science, especially those who desired to devote their lives to its work, could be informed as to its current advances. The need for a publication of some sort grew increasingly apparent, as the daily newspapers were showing more and more interest in Mrs. Eddy's work and were publishing inaccuracies that needed to be publicly corrected. Accordingly, Mrs. Eddy founded the *Journal of Christian Science* in 1883. Later the publication was called *The Christian Science Journal,* under which name it continues today. It was issued monthly and served Mrs. Eddy and her pupils in broadening their audience, "for it reaches a vast number of earnest readers, and seekers after Truth." (*Miscellaneous Writings,* p. 156)

The publication aided greatly in holding united the steadily increasing number of believers and in passing its Christian word to remote parts of the world. It proved to be a medium which aided in the long-run growth of Christian Science. In Boston the church services contributed greatly in promoting its immediate popularity, the attendance often exceeding the capacity of the hall.

There is no doubt that Mrs. Eddy's personality and convincing reasoning did much to attract attendance and to win adherents, for the audiences were smaller when announcements were made in advance that some one other than herself was to deliver the sermon. Nevertheless, Mrs. Eddy sometimes delegated one of her students to deliver the sermon in her place, wanting to lessen the public dependence upon herself. Christian Science was an impersonal doctrine and it was her purpose that no human being be deified. She desired that the new doctrine, with proper presentation, win its own way. In following the history of Christian Science, one sees clearly how Mrs. Eddy increasingly insisted on self-effacement and progressively formulated plans to insure that the doctrine she was delivering would stand firmly without the support of any single human being.

The Journal of Christian Science proved a boon to its many subscribers, for it brought words of cheer and encouragement into their homes. Its articles inspired spiritual growth, with the consequent disappearance of ills brought on by erroneous thoughts. In the many homes the periodical reached, the families could leisurely scan its contents and discuss them at will, thereby indelibly registering in their minds the truth that was thus brought to them. Through the articles in the *Journal,* the Bible and *Science and Health with Key to the Scriptures* became intimate and helpful companions in many households.

The periodical had its growing pains, brought on by ill-advised editors, but from the beginning, under Mrs. Eddy's wise guidance, its growth was substantial and its subject matter steadily improved in its presentation. The paper's far-reaching circulation attracted attention in distant cities, with the result that prospective students began to arrive in Boston from western points. When these students had completed their training and become sufficiently well-versed in Mind-healing, they returned to their home towns, where they set themselves up as Christian Science practitioners and availed themselves of the prestige which would be afforded them by displaying their cards as practitioners in the pages of *The Christian Science Journal.*

Further interest was stimulated as the circulation of the periodical became larger. Christian Science was becoming firmly established. Of course, there was still opposition to it; it had plenty of enemies. Some of the orthodox clergy denounced Christian Science vigorously, and some members of the medical profession were equally vituperative. Answering attacks took a good deal of Mrs. Eddy's valuable time, but she was deeply concerned with correcting misstatements and placing the infallibility of Christian Science on the record. Yet, although uncompromising in her answers, her heart remained full of love. It was with the attacks on her beliefs in mind that she wrote:

> Who is thine enemy that thou shouldst love him? Is it a creature or a thing outside thine own creation?
>
> Can you see an enemy, except you first formulate this enemy and then look upon the object of your own conception? What is it that harms you? Can height, or depth, or any other creature separate you from the Love that is omnipresent good,—that blesses infinitely one and all?
>
> Simply count your enemy to be that which defiles, defaces, and dethrones the Christ-image that you should reflect. Whatever purifies, sanctifies, and consecrates human life, is not an enemy, however much we suffer in the process. Shakespeare writes: "Sweet are the uses of adversity." Jesus said: "Blessed are ye, when men shall revile you, and persecute you, and shall say all manner of evil against you *falsely,* for my sake; . . . for so persecuted they the prophets which were before you."
>
> (*Miscellaneous Writings,* p. 8)

A great lesson is given in the foregoing lines, a lesson in true Christian Science. Questions are asked and answered, and the answers are crystal clear to spiritual minds, those enriched with an understanding of the new doctrine. One's own answers to the questions should reveal the truth, but Mrs. Eddy generously offers further assistance with her clear-cut statements.

Thus, it was the so-called enemies of Christian Science who, contrary to their intentions, were unknowingly testing and strengthening its teachings. Their purpose was to destroy but they were inadvertently building.

Mrs. Eddy had long known that so-called enemies helped her cause. She reasoned clearly: " 'Love thine enemies' is identical with 'Thou hast no enemies.' " She remembered well that Jesus said:

> Resist not him that is evil: but whosoever smiteth thee on the right cheek, turn to him the other also. And if any man would go to law with thee, and take away thy coat, let him have the cloak also.

Every thought of destroying the doctrine she was bringing to the world was cancelled by love and understanding. It was part of Mrs. Eddy's mission to bring all men together in brotherly love. She knew the wrong-doer was inherently good, but that he was ignorant and exerted his strength in a wrong direction. Further, she knew that it was possible for him to see the light of truth when his rancor had been spent and he came to understand that there was an all-governing power to which he should listen. "Whatever purifies, sanctifies, and consecrates human life, is not an enemy, however much we suffer in the process."

Although Mrs. Eddy worked hard to fit her students to carry forward the teachings and practice of Christian Science, and thus enable her to devote more of her time to writing, editorial work and the building up of the organization, there was no relaxation in the demands upon her personally. She stood out as the guiding spirit of Science healing, and there was no holding back the many seeking her help. Even students in distant cities craved her presence, and those in Chicago made a special plea that she honor their city and give classes and lectures in Christian Science there. Because of her many duties at headquarters, Mrs. Eddy was reluctant to leave Boston, even for a short period, but eventually the plea became so strong that she felt impelled to respond. Accordingly, in the spring of 1884, she left Boston for Chicago, accompanied by her secretary and a companion. Before leaving she temporarily suspended her Thursday night lectures and placed suitable substitutes in charge of the several branches of work she had been personally directing.

She spent a month in Chicago, where ample quarters were provided for her sizable classes. Great interest was shown in her subject; it attracted not only those who lived in Chicago, but many visitors from afar. Since it was not practical for her to speak individually with all those who sought her, she was invited to give a lecture in Hershey Hall. Upward of four hundred people attended and listened to her illuminating words. Her presence aroused tremendous interest, not only in Chicago but in the surrounding Midwest. Her spiritual personality deeply impressed all who heard and saw her, and did much to win many believers in the doctrine she expounded, and to raise in their hearts a desire to become Christian Scientists and to devote their lives to helping others by practicing Christian healing.

Following Mrs. Eddy's visit, Christian Science rapidly moved forward in the west. Newspapers and periodicals freely gave the subject space, it being a new topic to interest readers. They discussed its virtues or criticized and condemned it in no uncertain way. But Mrs. Eddy was alert and would not allow attacks to pass unchallenged. They were effectively answered in the columns of *The Christian Science Journal*. Interest in these published discussions grew and had the salient effect of increasing the circulation of the *Journal* by leaps and bounds. Those who read criticisms in the daily papers and national magazines would look for the replies in *The Christian Science Journal*. Thus, through these published criticisms and the replies made to them, the growth of Christian Science was unforeseeably stimulated. Mrs. Eddy's editorials in the *Journal* frequently could be regarded as sermons, for they set forth lessons which were inspiring and which stimulated spiritual growth in the reader.

When Mrs. Eddy returned to Boston, she must have been conscious that her doctrine was taking root firmly, and that the soil in the West was particularly fertile for its growth. The people in the open country were more receptive to new ideas than were those in the East, who were so infused with stereotyped orthodoxies.

There were many loyal and proficient students in Boston and vicinity who were now healing the sick, establishing harmony, and teaching others the Science of healing. Her use of the best of these students made it possible for Mrs. Eddy to broaden the horizon of Christian Science. Her confidence in them was sufficient to permit her to send several forth as disciples to distant cities, to teach and practice the new Science. New York City was not overlooked and she reached out as far as California. In all places the work was fruitful. There was constantly within her an urge to help her fellow man. Her words on this subject express how she felt and how practical she was in carrying out her desires:

> For many successive years I have endeavored to find new ways and means for the promotion and expansion of scientific Mind-healing, seeking to broaden its channels and, if possible, to build a hedge round about it that should shelter its perfections from the contaminating influences of those who have a small portion of its letter and less of its spirit. At the same time I have worked to provide a home for every true seeker and honest worker in this vineyard of Truth.
>
> To meet the broader wants of humanity, and provide folds for sheep that were without shepherds, I suggested to my students, in 1886, the propriety of forming a National Christian Scientist Association. This was immediately done, and delegates from the Christian Scientist Association of the Massachusetts Metaphysical College, and from branch associations in other States met in general convention at New York City, February 11, 1886.
>
> (*Retrospection and Introspection*, p. 52)

There is much significance in these words. Not only was it Mrs. Eddy's purpose to broaden the channels of scientific Mind-healing, but she clearly visualized the importance of protecting its tenets from contamination as well. This necessity was never overlooked in any of the successive steps taken in the advancement of Christian Science, and it is because this work was so well done that Christian Science became the enduring rock it is today.

Not least in Mrs. Eddy's mind was the desire "to provide a home for every true seeker and worker in this vineyard of Truth." How well she succeeded in this effort may be witnessed in reviewing the list of Christian Science practitioners and teachers contained each month in the *Christian Science Journal.* The names listed run into thousands upon thousands and are shown for all civilized parts of the world. All these people, who were once "seekers" are now "workers." They are lightening the burdens of their fellow men and, as a reward, they are enabled to provide for their homes and happiness. In all these thousands upon thousands, we can see hearts appreciative for the truth which had been taught them, and a lasting gratefulness to their great leader who brought them understanding. Increasing numbers are added each year to this vast world-wide army of Christian Science "workers." Thus, the good given to the world by Mrs. Eddy's work is so immense that it is beyond the capabilities of the human mind to appraise it. It is progressively increasing with the calendar and will continue to do so in future generations.

The healing of the sick is only a part of the good achieved through Mrs. Eddy's work. A large number of people have learned to understand and respect Christianity as they never did before, and to live exemplary Christian lives, lives without malice and filled with love for their fellow man.

One step leads to another and Mrs. Eddy always prepared the way for those steps that were before her. This foresight was evidenced throughout her life and is disclosed in her own words in the second paragraph last quoted. She did not impose her will upon her students but lovingly guided them in the next steps to be taken. "I suggested to my students, in 1886, the propriety of forming a National Christian Scientist Association." Here is to be seen the encouragement of teamwork along practical lines. By such methods, earnest workers, in response to the confidence shown them, put forth their best efforts. Mrs. Eddy had sown constructive thoughts; her students would cultivate and reap. The work was well done and Christian Science was organized on a national basis "to meet the broader wants of humanity" with an assurance of permanency. Several meetings were held and a tremendous step forward in stabilizing Christian Science had been achieved.

The Association continued its work until Mrs. Eddy deemed its purpose fulfilled and requested its members to adjourn. Her message was not for the present generation alone, but also for the generations which were to follow, and to be "forever reflected."

Nation-wide interest in Christian Science grew steadily. Colleges or centers of instruction came into existence in a great many cities and were the means of fulfilling the desires of many persons who sought to be instructed in the new doctrine. Meanwhile, in Boston, the Massachusetts Metaphysical College continued to flourish and to become increasingly popular. But the time came when Mrs. Eddy's perception told her that the Christian Science movement had outgrown the college, that the time had arrived for the church to rest on firmer foundations. Mrs. Eddy's own words are quoted in part:

> The apprehension of what has been, and must be, the final outcome of material organization, which wars with Love's spiritual compact, caused me to dread the unprecedented popularity of my College. Students from all over our continent, and from Europe, were flooding the school. At this time there were over three hundred applications from persons desiring to enter the College, and applicants were rapidly increasing. Example had shown the dangers arising from being placed on earthly pinnacles, and Christian Science shuns whatever involves material means for the promotion of spiritual ends.

In view of all this, a meeting was called of the Board of Directors of my College, who, being informed of my intentions, unanimously voted that the school be discontinued.

A Primary class student, richly imbued with the spirit of Christ, is a better healer and teacher than a Normal class student who partakes less of God's love.

(*Retrospection and Introspection,* p. 47)

The Board met October 29, 1889, and adopted a resolution to dissolve the corporation which had so usefully existed since it received its charter in 1881. The following was included in the minutes of the meeting:

Whereas, Other institutions for instruction in Christian Science, which are working out their periods of organization, will doubtless follow the example of the *Alma Mater* after having accomplished the worthy purpose for which they were organized, and the hour has come wherein the great need is for more of the spirit instead of the letter, and Science and Health is adapted to work this result;". . .

(*Retrospection and Introspection,* p. 49)

It would have required extreme courage on the part of any person other than Mrs. Eddy to close a college which was so prosperous and in such popular demand; but it did not require courage on Mrs. Eddy's part, for it was wisdom that guided her. She knew instinctively this was the proper step to take in the interest of her message, and that now was the time to take it. She knew that present successes did not, necessarily, presage their continuance and it was with the future that she was most concerned. Permanency was her objective and its achievement was being put into jeopardy by "being placed on earthly pinnacles."

"Material organization which wars with Love's spiritual compact" had to be used as a step to open the way, because in this earthly world the human equation must be enlisted as a vehicle for smoothing the path which reaches out to spiritual goals. But "material means," because of their impermanence, are incompatible with the ultimate achievement of "spiritual ends." Christian Science is best served by the admission of students impelled with fervent hearts who truly seek its teachings along spiritual lines and who gain their inspiration from the pages of *Science and Health*. This avenue was opened to all, everywhere in the world.

What was true of the Boston college—that it no longer served its purpose—would become equally so in respect to organized schools in other cities. Because the Board of Directors was aware of this, they included in their resolution the last paragraph quoted. Mrs. Eddy's foresight, as always, enabled her to direct the many steps in the evolution of her mission with the most consistent precision.

The increasing numbers of students brought increasing requests for copies of *Science and Health with Key to the Scriptures*. As many as fifteen editions had been printed, yet there were still an insufficient number of copies to meet the demand. Although Mrs. Eddy had steadily improved the clarity of her book with each printing, she now felt it necessary to revise further, amplify and elucidate some of its statements. In August, 1885, she completed this huge task and a short time later the sixteenth edition was printed by the University Press, Cambridge.

At all times Mrs. Eddy held to the belief that *Science and Health with Key to the Scriptures* was the most important means of imparting her message to truly faithful seekers. She writes:

> The hour has struck for Christian Scientists to do their own work; to appreciate the signs of the times; to demonstrate self-knowledge and self-government; and to demonstrate, as this period demands, over all sin, disease, and death. The dear ones whom I would have great pleasure in instructing, know that the door to my teaching was shut when my College was closed.
>
> Again, it is not absolutely requisite for some people

to be taught in a class, for they can learn by spiritual growth and by the study of what is written. Scarcely a moiety, compared with the whole of the Scriptures and the Christian Science textbook, is assimilated spiritually by the most faithful seekers; yet this assimilation is indispensable to the progress of every Christian Scientist.

(Miscellaneous Writings, p. 317)

Mrs. Eddy was sure of her ground, of the Bible, of her textbook. She was certain that when they were studied together, with the textbook used as a "Key to the Scriptures," spiritual growth would be the reward of all true seekers. The work she had accomplished now made it possible for seekers to gain the enlightenment they desired without the aid of academic instruction. Spiritual growth would be measured by their earnestness, sincerity and willingness to study hard and long and by their ability to demonstrate that which they had learned. Successful demonstration would only be possible for those who had learned well the truth of Christian Science.

CHAPTER

18

THE TIME WAS NOW approaching for the third annual convention of the National Christian Scientist Association. It was decided it would be held in Chicago because it was an important railroad center offering students easy access from all parts of the country. It was quite natural that Mrs. Eddy should be urged to be present at such an important meeting—one which she was especially desirous of being well attended. Again she found it difficult to comply because of the many duties demanding her time at home. But one who is anxious to serve God always finds a way. The example of the Master was there for Mrs. Eddy to follow. He was no recluse; He was always among people where God's work is best done. When He resorted to solitude it was for the purpose of regeneration and communion with the Holy Spirit, enabling Him to return to His task strengthened by the light He had so received. During Mrs. Eddy's formative childhood days, intervals of solitude were an essential foundation for her future work. Now that those days were over, and she was well launched in her mission, it became her duty to be, as much as practicable, in the midst of God's children.

It is interesting to note how John Wesley, passing through a stage of uncertainty, was awakened to the course he should pursue. Arnold Lunn, in his book on John Wesley writes:

> From the fens of Lincolnshire, Wesley returned with a new attitude of religion. He had hoped to save his soul as a recluse, only to learn from a "serious person" whom he had met by chance in the country that he was on the wrong side of salvation.

"Sir, you wish to serve God and go to Heaven,"
the "serious person" had said, "remember you cannot
serve Him alone, you must try to find companions or
make them. The Bible knows nothing of solitary religion."

A few words will sometimes alter a man's whole outlook. These words sunk into Wesley and became the
motto of his life.

There had been no need of a "serious person" or any other
person to impart to Mrs. Eddy the necessity of mingling with
her fellow man. It had long been her wisdom to do so. She had
been and still was sacrificing her strength in order to carry on
the great amount of writing she had to do, in addition to the
teaching, healing, lectures, sermons, personal interviews, and
moments of communion. Her capacity for work was tremendous
and she never became confused.

Eight hundred delegates met in Chicago's Central Music Hall
but, because of the wide publicity given the convention by the
newspapers, the announcement attracted many others who were
not Christian Scientists. Without Mrs. Eddy's permission, it was
announced that she would be present. Consequently, the hall
was filled to overflowing, with more than four thousand people
present. Mrs. Eddy had not been informed until her arrival at
the Hall that she would be called upon to deliver the main
address. It came to her as a surprise for she had not prepared
herself for such a part. The Reverend George B. Day had withheld telling her until the last minute because it was feared she
would withhold her consent, preferring that others carry forward
the ceremonies of the meeting.

When Mrs. Eddy appeared on the platform, the audience
spontaneously rose to its feet and remained standing in silent
tribute until motioned to be seated. The presence of this great
leader had moved over four thousand souls to rise as one man,
without premeditation, in expression of the high regard and love
they felt for the woman who stood before them. At this moment
Mrs. Eddy was surely conscious of God; conscious of God, All-

in-all; conscious that all those before her were God's children, He in them and they in Him. She felt herself to be in the presence of harmony, in the presence of love, and that she, as God's messenger, had been sent to unite these children with a spiritual message. They were gathered here together in one thought, to hear God's word from one whom He dearly loved. The moment was supreme. Silence expressed God's presence in the hearts of all.

It was fortunate that Mrs. Eddy had come without a prepared address. For a prepared address, no matter how carefully planned, could never have fitted an occasion such as this, where each and everyone was unconscious of self. Nothing could reach these hearts save that which emanated from the heart. Even the newspaper reporters became so infused with the spiritual atmosphere that they forgot to make full notes of the speaker's words.

Mrs. Eddy was composed and radiant. Her eyes looked upward, as though seeking divine guidance, as she was wont to do. Then, in a clear and cultured voice, which reached all corners of the auditorium, she recited the first verse of the ninety-first Psalm:

"He that dwelleth in the secret place of the most High shall abide under the shadow of the Almighty."

That which followed is beautifully told by Julia Michael Johnson in *Mary Baker Eddy: Her Mission and Triumph*:

> Without hesitancy or apparent effort, without a single preparatory note, this text was unfolded into a disclosure which held her audience enthralled. It was as though "the glory of the Lord shone round about them." It was this sense of God with her that touched the deepest feelings of men and women, held the pencils of the reporters still, and left an inerasable memory with her listeners.

Mrs. Eddy spoke at great length. It was not an address, although reported to be such; it was not a sermon; it was not a lecture. It was an effervescence of spiritual revelation translated into words for human understanding, words that marshalled thoughts which inspired all hearers to join in God's work. They were words which "left an inerasable memory with her listeners." The speaker was conscious that her words would project into the future for she told her hearers:

> In no other one thing seemed Jesus of Nazareth more divine than in His faith in the immortality of His words. He said "Heaven and earth shall pass away, but my words shall not pass away"; and they have not. The winds of time sweep clean the centuries, but they can never bear into oblivion His words. They still live, and tomorrow speak louder than today. They are as the voice of one crying in the wilderness, "Make straight God's paths; make way for health, holiness, universal harmony, and come up hither." The grandeur of the word, the power of Truth, is again casting out evils and healing the sick; and it is whispered, "This is Science."
>
> Jesus taught by the wayside, in humble homes. He spoke of Truth and Love to artless listeners and dull disciples. His immortal words were articulated in a decaying language, and then left to the providence of God. Christian Science was to interpret them; and woman, "last at the cross," was to awaken the dull senses, intoxicated with pleasure or pain, to the infinite meaning of those words.
>
> <div align="right">(<i>Miscellaneous Writings,</i> pp. 99-100,
Extract of Address)</div>

Jesus' words have been heard for two thousand years. Although "He spake in a decaying language," His words today are heard in all languages of the world and those who hear them grow in numbers for each year added to the calendar of time. So it is with Mrs. Eddy's words. Already they are heard in many languages of the world and those who hear them are growing in number. Jesus' words came to the world from God. He repeatedly told us this truth. Mrs. Eddy's words, likewise, must

have come into the world from God. She must be just as truly
God's messenger as Jesus is God's beloved Son.

Again quoting Mrs. Eddy's words:

> The Christian Scientist loves man more because he
> loves God most. He understands this Principle,—Love.
> (*Miscellaneous Writings*, p. 100)

How this statement must have impressed her audience, hearing her utter it with the exultation of love. A tremendous obliga-
tion is placed on the shoulders of Christian Scientists because
Mrs. Eddy's words are framed as a statement of fact; a statement
that cannot be lightly passed by; a statement that every Christian
Scientist is expected to live up to every day of his life. Each
one must be grateful when he feels within him this God-given
principle; and the unfortunate one who has been unsuccessful
in acquiring it must be sad indeed. But for such a one there is
still hope, although his path is not easy. With sincerity and
diligence it will be possible for the spirit of love to enter his
heart.

These important words must not be overlooked just because
they numbered only sixteen of an address of from three to four
thousand words that was delivered by the speaker. They should
especially be remembered because they disclose the great good
given to the world through Christian Science. Those who are
infused with this high principle will progressively impart it
to others and so the spirit of brotherly love will spread till the
world knows strife no longer.

Love was the keynote of Mrs. Eddy's whole life. It has been
shown in these pages how, as she progressed through life, she
expressed love in all her work and imparted the divine principle
to her students, so that they could live accordingly and in turn
teach others as they themselves had been taught.

At a later point in her address, Mrs. Eddy again brings to the
attention of her audience the importance of love to Christian
Science.

> In obedience to divine nature, man's individuality
> reflects the divine law and order of being. How shall we

reach our true selves? Through Love. The Principle of Christian Science is Love, and its idea represents Love. This divine Principle and idea are demonstrated, in healing, to be God and the real man.

(Miscellaneous Writings, p. 104)

Those in the audience who took time to reflect upon these words must have discerned how truly scientific the first sentence was. Upon close analysis, the meaning of her statement could not be controverted. She points very clearly in her own words to what Jesus told His hearers when He said:

"The Kingdom of God cometh not with observation. Neither shall they say, *Lo here or, lo, there!* For the Kingdom of God is within you" (Luke 17: 20-21).

Then all yearning hearts are told "how to reach their true selves."

Mrs. Eddy's whole address was replete with the principles upon which Christian Science is founded; each sentence was clear and concise and filled with undeniable truth. Before concluding, Mrs. Eddy spoke as follows and then, with a bit of humor, recited the verse which is repeated here:

Christian Science and Christian Scientists will, *must*, have a history; and if I could write the history in poor parody on Tennyson's grand verse, it would read thus:—

Traitors to right of them,
M.D.'s to left of them,
Priestcraft in front of them,
    Volleyed and thundered!
Into the jaws of hate,
Out through the door of Love,
On to the blest above,
    Marched the one hundred.

(Miscellaneous Writings, p. 106)

This verse good-naturedly reflects the vicissitudes through which Christian Science had traveled and was traveling, and indicated how it was emerging "through the door of Love." With equal verity Mary could have quoted David in his reply to Goliath when the former was challenged in combat by the giant Philistine:

> Then said David to the Philistine, Thou comest to me with sword, and spear, and with a shield; but I come to thee in the name of the Lord of hosts, the God of the armies of Israel, whom thou has defied. This day will the Lord deliver thee into mine hand; and I will smite thee, and take thine head from thee, and I will give the carcases of the host of the Philistines this day unto the fowls of the air, and to the wild beasts of the earth; that all the earth may know that there is a God in Israel. And this assembly shall know that the lord saveth not sword and spear; for the battle is the Lord's, and he will give you into our hands. (Samuel 17:45, 46, 47)

The unmerciful opposition to Mrs. Eddy's message and to her personally came from many directions and persisted to the end of her mortal life. But she stood her ground against all who "volleyed and thundered," and met their onslaughts with reason and love.

It is significant that she stated that Christian Science and Christian Scientists "will and *must* have a history." This is a declaration and a prophecy which already has abundantly been fulfilled and will be added to with advancing years.

The acclaim given Mrs. Eddy at the conclusion of her address was tremendous. The whole audience rose and crowded the platform where she was standing. Many people attempted to tell her their stories of how they had been healed by reading her book *Science and Health*. She received this homage silently and at last was led, with much difficulty, through the crowds to her carriage.

At her hotel, people of all walks in life gathered in her honor. Although unprepared for this, her gracious manner did not desert her, and she appeared before her enthusiastic callers.

But it was evident to her friends that she was conscious that such a display of personal worship did not conform to the principles of Christian Science. She felt strongly that steps must be taken to correct this error of thought in the minds of those who would further the interest of her teachings.

A year later a similar ovation was given Mrs. Eddy when she addressed the Christian Science Conference in Steinway Hall, New York. This gave her further evidence that it was not possible to escape personal adoration unless she removed herself from direct participation in public affairs and that, in the interest of Christian Science, it was essential for her to do so.

CHAPTER

19

THE CLOSING OF THE MASSACHUSETTS Metaphysical College, the disbanding of the Boston Church organization, and Mrs. Eddy's withdrawal from public activities were all in the interest of the progress of Christian Science, which could not benefit by a dictator. Its whole emphasis was on principle, not on individuals. Mrs. Eddy's withdrawal, therefore, showed her wisdom and keen understanding of God's law. She would have no part in personal adulation.

Seeking a location where she would be less available to her students, Mrs. Eddy decided on Barre, Vermont. This proved unsuitable to her needs, however, and she moved to a residence in Roslindale, a suburb of Boston. But Roslindale was too accessible to the many who wished to see her, and she did not remain there long. Concord, New Hampshire, near her old home town, appealed to Mrs. Eddy as offering the accommodations best suited to her needs. There she could enjoy the privacy so necessary to her work and yet be near enough to Boston to keep in touch with the activities she was directing there. Accordingly, she rented a furnished house, where she lived until she had built a home of her own, a modest modern house on the outskirts of Concord. Mrs. Eddy named the house Pleasant View and lived there for about fifteen years.

At Pleasant View Mrs. Eddy could lead a simple existence, labor at God's work, and breathe the essence of His Creation. She was free at last of the adulation which her grateful admirers had sought to force on her. Luxury and glorification were not for God's messenger, whose message to mankind was impersonal in character. She had but one purpose, to be true to her mission. The truth taught by Jesus was no longer understood; it had not been for many generations. There was need of some one to come forward to reveal its full meaning.

In withdrawing from the midst of personal acclaim, however, Mrs. Eddy was in no way abandoning her field work. On the contrary, she was strengthening it because, being at a distance from its main arteries, her perspective was clearer, enabling her to direct its activities with keener perspicacity. At the same time, her followers developed self-reliance by having to work alone, without leaning directly upon their leader. They had her written works to guide them, and the study of these would give them spiritual understanding.

Guided by her convictions, Mrs. Eddy wrote to the president of the National Christian Science Association, recommending that the Association be dissolved. She pointed out that it was now in the interest of Christian Science that the members of the Association work out the problems of life individually. As free children of God, who had given them spiritual understanding, they might assemble together and evolve plans that would insure a unity of purpose.

In the quiet of her home, freed from the merciless demand for personal interviews, Mrs. Eddy was now able to devote much time to perfecting the organization which was to place her doctrine on a firm foundation. Her message had been brought to light, but there was the danger that in the course of time it would be lost sight of in the turmoil of human activities, and that eventually its beneficent influence might fall into oblivion. It was Mrs. Eddy's mission not only to deliver the message entrusted to her, but to place it firmly in the world where it would abide with mankind forever. This task was before her. She had long been conscious that it should be done, and already she had made a good beginning.

In *Miscellaneous Writings*, p. 370, Mrs. Eddy says:

> In different ages the divine idea assumes different forms, according to humanity's needs. In this age it assumes, more intelligently than ever before, the form of

Christian healing. This is the babe we are to cherish.
This is the babe that twines its loving arms about the
neck of omnipotence, and calls forth infinite care from
His loving heart.

The divine idea of this age is surely Christian healing. Men
today are better prepared to understand the nothingness of matter and the unreality of evil than ever before. Physical science
is now bringing this great truth to light, and corroborates Mrs.
Eddy's teachings in a most remarkable and convincing way. Yet
it is essential that it never be forgotten that God is All-in-all, that
God is Mind, therefore Mind is All-in-all. It is essential that
God's message, given in Mrs. Eddy's *Science and Health with
Key to the Scriptures,* continue to serve man in future ages.

Mrs. Eddy never lost sight of her students' needs. She encouraged them to organize local churches all over the country.
This made it possible for detached organizations to plan their
local needs within the scope of their circumstances. This is a
truly healthy and sane system, one by which local interest and
local pride contribute much to stability.

Mrs. Eddy, always meticulous in every detail of her work,
desired uniformity of procedure in the conduct of her churches
throughout the world, which were always increasing in number.
Therefore, by-laws were prepared to guide trustees and the
Christian Science Board of Directors in administering the affairs of the church. Also, church by-laws were adopted to govern the conduct of all churches and members. These by-laws
were incorporated in a manual for ready reference. They are
complete in all details and are constructively helpful in every
way. Through this instrument, it was made possible for Christian Scientists to unite in church services and Wednesday evening meetings in any part of the world, knowing that they were
following the rules given them by their great leader and, at the
same time, retaining the freedom of local self-government. The
purity of Mrs. Eddy's teachings must never be departed from if
Christian Science is to continue into the future.

The members of the Christian Science Board of Directors

were selected or approved by Mrs. Eddy. They were Christian Scientists of proved worth, of high caliber and administrative ability. The Board constituted a permanent and central government for all activities of the Church and, in the latter years of Mrs. Eddy's life, did much to relieve her of the many details so necessary to its functioning. Publication work, alone, was growing to huge proportions, and came under the administration of The Christian Science Publishing Society, headed by a Board of Trustees. In order to secure accuracy and quality in its publications, it became desirable for the Society to establish its own printing plant. Therefore, Mrs. Eddy gave the Board of Trustees a deed of trust for property on which to erect a suitable plant.

Notwithstanding these up-to-date and efficient organizations, Mrs. Eddy did not relinquish her own participation in the progress of the Church movement. She worked long hours each day at her Pleasant View home, where literature and documents of all sorts pertaining to Church affairs were sent to her for review and criticism. No details were neglected, no matter how voluminous the subject and the papers were returned with corrections and advice.

The administrative officers benefited much by this supervision of their work, for their leader's judgment proved always to be right. With each experience, these officers learned to better understand Mrs. Eddy's way of thinking and to be governed accordingly. While already possessed of a goodly understanding of Christian Science and its divine principle, there was a progressive enhancement in the knowledge they so gained.

It was definitely Mrs. Eddy's purpose to improve the understanding of her officers to the highest possible degree, in order to enable them to direct the affairs of the Church properly and, in due time, to train others to succeed them. These loyal officers are imbued with spiritual understanding and brotherly love, and carry on their work with the God-given proficiency they are enabled to demonstrate through earnestly following the Science of Christianity as set forth in the revelation of their leader.

In the establishment of her church organization, Mrs. Eddy

forged an indestructible structure, one which will endure through the years of time. This is no idle statement. Although Mrs. Eddy has been gone for forty years at this writing, the purity of her message has in no way been diluted and is being effectively carried to all parts of the world. The structure she built is being added to progressively, without change in its form, and is gaining in stability.

A better idea of how untiringly Mrs. Eddy labored cannot be had than that which is given by that most eminent clergyman, the Rev. Irving C. Tomlinson, M.A., C.S.B., in his book, *Twelve Years With Mary Baker Eddy*, p. 111. His words are quoted here:

> Any examination of Mrs. Eddy's activities as an author must of necessity be inadequate. The mere recounting of the facts can never tell of the earnest labor, of the consecrated prayer which she gave to the preparation of her monumental works. Up to the closing of her College, in a single day she often taught a class, interviewed students, settled knotty church problems, and then, while others were sleeping, wrote far into the night, laboring long and arduously to give the precise interpretation of God's Word which might be needed to convince the reader of the truth of Christian Science. Early the next morning she would be at her desk, dictating to her secretary the stirring words of some one of her works before the gathering of the class.
>
> Stopping to call one afternoon on her drive in Concord, New Hampshire, she told me that she had been at work the night before until four o'clock in the morning. After all this labor, to her fell the task of correcting mistakes of typists, printers, and proof readers. How little the world knows, how slightly it appreciates, the hardships and self-sacrifice of Mary Baker Eddy in presenting her inspired revelation to the sons of men! Only through divine wisdom and unceasing toil did

she accomplish the work of keeping Christian Science unadulterated. What humanity owes to her foresight in establishing The Christian Science Publishing Society, it now little comprehends, but future ages will accord a just estimate to the untiring labor and manifold achievements of the Founder of the Christian Science movement.

These words of the Rev. Irving C. Tomlinson cannot be repeated too often. The world has reason indeed to be grateful for the fruit of Mrs. Eddy's labors, which were given so unsparingly.

The original Boston church, which operated under a charter obtained in 1879, was reorganized in 1892, and has continued ever since then under a special set of by-laws which Mrs. Eddy adopted for the reorganized Boston church. At the time of reorganization, its name was changed to *The First Church of Christ Scientist* and it is known as The Mother Church. Members of local churches, all over the world, may, if they desire, also be members of the Mother Church. Many avail themselves of this privilege; thus the unification of Christian Science is further promoted.

In these moves it is again plainly evident that Mrs. Eddy was always ready to advance when the right time came. It was never too much labor for her to make changes, if they would result in important strides in the accomplishment of her mission. In later years, after the teachings of Christian Science had been well formulated, she was divinely guided in establishing its teachings and its purity on a permanent basis, in order that mankind might be given its benefits for generations to come.

The Christian Science Church had now been set on an unshakable foundation. Mrs. Eddy had eliminated the possibility of conflicting personalities by liberating the church from personal preachings and, in lieu thereof, ordained the Bible and *Science and Health with Key to the Scriptures* as pastors for the Mother Church and all branch churches. These, the Bible and *Science and Health with Key to the Scriptures*, were to

be read by First and Second Readers, and the Sunday lessons
from these two holy books selected from the Christian Science
Quarterly. The effectiveness and understanding of the lessons
recited at the Sunday services are increased by daily readings
by its members of the lessons selected for the ensuing Sunday.

An organization of this kind had been unheard of in all
church history. A unique gift had been made to the Christian
Science Church, yes, to Christianity. It is Christianity which
the Christian Science Church teaches, and Christianity has its
source in the Bible. What could be more logical then, than
to assign first place to that Holy Book as an impersonal preacher
of its teachings? It was difficult at the time for Mrs. Eddy's
followers to believe that this new system was workable. But
they had faith in their leader and accepted it. Time has since
proven how truly Mrs. Eddy interpreted God's voice.

Science and Health with Key to the Scriptures had taken
many years in its evolution. Many tedious hours were occupied
in writing and rewriting it. In the interest of her mission, Mrs.
Eddy spent endless hours in solitude and communion with
God in search of divine guidance.

This wonderful book is not a book any more than the Bible
is a book. The latter may be regarded as a collection of books,
or to be more exact, a collection of truths or lessons divinely
handed down to man for his ethical guidance. The Bible in-
forms us that all Scripture is given by inspiration of God.
Therefore, its pages should be read with humility and faith in
God's word, with a desire to understand His meaning. Only
by careful study is it possible to breathe the truths contained
in its inspired pages. Because the lessons between its covers
are endless in number, one cannot glean their many truths
by sequentially reading its pages as one does an ordinary book.
To read it from cover to cover is to miss much of its meaning.
Conversely, to read *Science and Health* in fragments is also to
miss much of its meaning. The work deserves comprehensive
study as an entire book, as well as particularized study of its individual statements.

It is a blessing that this inspired book may be opened at

random, and lo!—on the page thus unfolded there will be revealed lessons of spiritual worth! Each page is worthy of careful
and devout study, impelled by a will to gather its inspired meanings. The Bible is a theological treasure, accessible at all
times to those who truly desire to gather the wealth it has
to offer. No man can be too lowly to benefit by the rewards
there awaiting him. It is a God-given book, given to His children that they may look above earthly things to gain the
meanings of spiritual thoughts and thus be invested with the
Holy Ghost. This precious storehouse is there for all who
wish to gather the worthwhile things in life. Each reader can
fill his heart with divine love from its overflowing pages.

How well we all realize that the Bible has a mission of
infinite importance to man; that its pages are replete with
infinite wisdom, reflecting the good God offers to His children,
reflecting infinite love; filling the hearts of men with faith,
hope and charity! These pages were centuries in their making,
and nearly twenty centuries have elapsed since their completion.
Every year, since that time, these pages have became the companion of more and more men. The world has seen many
changes in that interval of time, many vicissitudes have been
experienced and many advances made in the physical sciences,
yet the pages of the Bible rest firmly on the rock of ages, and
still retain their original purity, progressively serving more
men as each century is added to the preceding one. With each
year added to history, more and more people gain a clearer
perception of the teaching of the Holy Scriptures than in preceding years, thus definitely proving that their mission is for the
benefit of man for all time. In *Miscellany*, p. 295, Mrs. Eddy
says:

> Christian Scientists are fishers of men. The Bible
> is our sea-beaten rock. It guides the fishermen. It stands
> the storm. It engages the attention and enriches the
> being of all men.

It was this sublime book that so clearly held Mrs. Eddy's
attention from her early childhood till the time of her departure

from this mortal world. She wrote in *Science and Health,*
p. 110: "In following these leadings of scientific revelations,
the Bible was my only textbook."

In recorded history it is difficult to find anyone who was a
more devout student of the Bible than Mrs. Eddy. She carefully
and prayerfully studied its every page. Her familiarity and keen
understanding of its teachings are fully revealed in her writings,
and were repeatedly disclosed through her numerous lectures
and sermons, many delivered without notes.

Like the Bible, *Science and Health with Key to the Scriptures*
cannot be regarded as a book in the ordinary sense of the word.
It may be opened haphazardly and a lesson in truth will be revealed. Each page conveys a message that is an inspiration to
the understanding reader. The keynote of this remarkable book
is Christian healing, divinely evolved through interpretations
of the Scriptures. Its purpose is to help students in Christian
Science and, when used accordingly, its pages, even when taken
separately, offer fundamental lessons, complete in themselves.
They bring into view the allness of God and the nothingness
of matter. The basis of Mrs. Eddy's reasoning which flows
through *Science and Health* is briefly stated on page 468:

> *Question*:   What is the scientific statement of being?
> *Answer*:   There is no life, truth, intelligence, nor
>   substance in matter. All is infinite Mind
>   and its infinite manifestation, for God is
>   All-in-all. Spirit is immortal Truth; mat-
>   ter is unreal and temporal. Matter is mor-
>   tal error. Spirit is the real and eternal;
>   Spirit is God, and man is His image and
>   likeness. Therefore man is not material;
>   he is spiritual.

In these lines we are able to see why she used the words
"Mind-healing" so freely when referring to Christian healing.
Her scientific statement of being is supported by numerous
other statements. That which follows and which is quoted from

page 469 of *Science and Health*, may be of particular interest
here:

> *Question*:   What is Mind?
> *Answer*:   Mind is God. The exterminator of error
>   is the great truth that God, good, is the
>   *only* Mind, and that the suppositious op-
>   posite of infinite Mind—called *devil* or
>   evil—is not Mind, is not Truth, but error,
>   without intelligence or reality. There can
>   be but one Mind, because there is but one
>   God; and if mortals claimed no other Mind
>   and accepted no other, sin would be un-
>   known. We can have but one Mind, if
>   that one is infinite.

Mrs. Eddy was insistent in all her writings on making it
clear that there is but one Mind—God. She also made it clear
that the Bible was her only textbook and that the great truth
therein was divinely revealed to her. These brief quotations,
extracted from the seven hundred closely printed pages of
Science and Health, convey some idea of the enormity of her
works and of the invaluable lessons contained therein. She writes
on page 319:

> The divine Science taught in the original language
> of the Bible came through inspiration, and needs in-
> spiration to be understood. Hence the misapprehension
> of the spiritual meaning of the Bible, and the misinter-
> pretation of the Word in some instances by uninspired
> writers, who only wrote down what an inspired teacher
> had said. A misplaced word changes the sense and
> misstates the Science of the Scriptures, as, for instance,
> to name Love as merely an attribute of God; but we
> can by special and proper capitalization speak of the
> love of Love, meaning by that what the beloved disciple
> meant in one of his epistles, when he said "God is
> Love." Likewise we can speak of the truth of Truth

and of the life of Life, for Christ plainly declared,
"I am the way, the truth, and the life."

This statement is of exceeding importance in weighing the
value of *Science and Health* and her many other writings.
Those who study her sublime gift need to do so in a spirit of
holiness, a feeling of oneness with the Father-Mother-God.
That Mrs. Eddy was ever conscious of being divinely led, when
writing *Science and Health* is emphasized by her own words in
Miscellany, page 114:

> My first writings on Christian Science began with
> notes on the Scriptures. I consulted no other book but
> the Bible for three years. What I wrote had a strange
> coincidence or relationship with light of revelation and
> solar light. I could not write these notes after sunset.
> All thoughts in line of Scriptural interpretation would
> leave me until the rising of the sun. Then the influx
> of divine interpretation would pour in upon my spir-
> itual sense as gloriously as the sunlight on the material
> senses. It was not myself, but the divine power of
> Truth and Love, infinitely above me, which dictated
> *Science and Health with Key to the Scriptures.* I have
> been learning the higher meaning of this book since
> writing it.

From these thoughts one is made aware more than ever of
how these two books are so closely bound together.

Truth—the allness of God and the nothingness of matter—
logically supports every and each of the many subjects dealt
with in *Science and Health*. The reader is provided with overwhelming proof of the soundness of the theology upon which
Christian Science is founded. A brief example of clarity, con-
ciseness and consistency is found in the Glossary of *Science
and Health*, page 591:

> MIND. The only I, or Us; the only Spirit, Soul,
> divine Principle, substance, Life, Truth, Love; the
> one God; not that which is in man, but the divine

Principle, or God, of whom man is the full and perfect expression, Deity, which outlines but is not outlined.

Greater meaning could not be compressed into so few words as in those just quoted. No eulogy, no matter how great and sincere, is able to convey a full idea of the spiritual worth of Mrs. Eddy's inspired book. Perhaps the most practical measure of its value to mankind may be obtained by viewing its popularity. During Mrs. Eddy's lifetime, upwards of 380 editions were printed and sold. New printings in endless procession are continuing to flow from the presses of The Christian Science Publishing Society, and will do so for a long time to come.

Hundreds of thousands of Christian Scientists and tens of thousands of Christian Science practitioners value their copies beyond any of their material possessions. These copies are read diligently each day with the weekly Bible lesson designated in the Christian Science Quarterly. *Science and Health* influences hundreds of thousands of men and women all over the world and helps them to live exemplary and happy lives and to be the best of citizens. Good health, harmony, and self-reliance are brought into their lives; uplifting hopes and new interests replace moments of uncertainty and despair. They understand love in its fullest meaning—God—and serenely radiate this divine attribute among those who come near them.

"Believe me that I am in the Father, and the Father in me; or else believe me for the very works' sake." (John 14:11)

Jesus' words may be justly paraphrased: Believe Mary Baker Eddy that she is in God, and God in her; or else believe her for her very works' sake.

The evidence of the truth of this statement is irrefutable. It is to be found everywhere, in nearby and far distant countries. All through Mrs. Eddy's life, repeated evidence has substantiated the belief that there was a divine influence governing her thoughts and her works, and now that she has so faithfully delivered her message to the world, we see how she had been "set apart for wonderful achievements." We see in her works a beneficent gift to mankind, a practical influence and guide for good. We judge her message by the good it achieves; we judge Mary Baker Eddy by her works. We cannot forget her declaration when but a small child: "I shall write a book." Neither can we forget the prophecy made by the Rev. Enoch Corser: "She has some great future, mark that." Not least are we impressed by the overwhelming fruits of her labors. Thousands upon thousands of men and women, the world over, bear witness to this in their testimony of healing, happiness and a higher aim in life gained through embracing Christian Science.

"Herein is my Father glorified, that ye bear much fruit; so shall ye be my disciples." (John 15:8)

CHAPTER

20

F OR SEVERAL YEARS it had been the wish of the members of the Boston Church to have a church edifice of their own. In January, 1895, the completion and dedication of this new church were achieved. In this new edifice personal preaching was omitted. Reading from the Bible and *Science and Health with Key to the Scriptures* took the place of a pastor's sermon.

There was much public interest in the new building, particularly among Christian Scientists. Newspapers all over the country commented upon it, regarding the event as an important one. They reported that the membership of the Boston Church exceeded four thousand.

When the cornerstone was laid at the beginning of the construction of the church, an address prepared by Mrs. Eddy was read before those officiating at the ceremony. Her address was lengthy and concluded with the following words:

> To The Church of Christ, Scientist, in Boston, and to the dear children that my heart folds within it, let me say, "Tis sweet to remember thee, and God's Zion, with healing wings. May her walls be vocal with salvation; and her gates with praise!"

The concluding sentences show deep spiritual sentiment. They reflect the great leader's heartfelt thoughts, which were inspired by love. She was not present at this ceremony, nor at the dedication when the church was finished and opened for Sunday services. Her absence on these important occasions reflects how earnestly Mrs. Eddy adhered to her resolve to evade personal adulation.

Furthermore, she need not be present in person to bring her works into being. Sustained by unbending self-reliant strength, her prayers, her thoughts, her words, were in unity with all-creation. God's children, understanding His Law, could bring into reality the words she had delivered.

To Mrs. Eddy this first church edifice represented the embodiment of life. ". . May *her* walls . . . and *her* gates . . .", reflect this thought. It was the creation of the Mind in fulfillment of divine purpose. Within *her* walls would be heard the voice of the Holy Bible and that of *Science and Health with Key to the Scriptures*. It was spiritually conceived and would be so used.

Several months after the dedication of the church edifice, the Christian Science Board of Directors, in behalf of the First Church of Christ, Scientist, Boston, Massachusetts, presented their church edifice to Mary Baker Eddy as a testimonial of the Church's love and gratitude. Mrs. Eddy graciously declined to accept this wonderful gift. Although it was a monument to her work, she again sensed that personality was no part of God's will. The edifice was for the use of His children and could not, without violating His law, become the property of a single child.

When, years before, Mrs. Eddy had told George Clark that she would have a church of her own some day, she did not mean that she would become the owner of a church building. Her words had a spiritual meaning. The church building she was viewing at the time was used to exemplify, through its material form, church congregations who would assemble in Christian Science services; congregations which would be governed by her teachings as revealed to her by the Holy Spirit. In this, her prophecy has been fulfilled, and in a very large way.

A decade later, after an extension to the Mother Church had been completed and dedicated, Mary Baker Eddy graciously reiterated her wish for self-effacement in the following notice, quoted from the First Church of Christ, Scientist, and *Miscellany*:

To the Beloved Members of my Church, The Mother Church, The First Church of Christ, Scientist, in Boston:—Divine Love bids me say: Assemble not at the residence of your Pastor Emeritus at or about the time of our annual meeting and communion service, for the divine and not the human should engage our attention at this sacred season of prayer and praise.

No heart could have been more sincere than that of Mary Baker Eddy in her resolve to discourage the personal devotion of her many loving followers. She desired them to be Christian Scientists in the true meaning of its teachings; to know that there is but one Mind-God, and that He alone was the One to whom gratitude should be given. Her part in the great revelation was only that of a messenger in the service of her Divine Master.

When one looks back upon the time when the extension was made to the Mother Church in Boston, the saintly character of Mary Baker Eddy becomes increasingly clear. The addition to the Church was monumental in all respects. An imposing and beautiful temple had been given to the world, one so grand that words cannot adequately describe it. *The Boston Post* of June 6, 1906, wrote in part:

> The services of Sunday will mark an epoch in the history of Christian Science. Since the discovery by Mrs. Eddy, many beautiful houses of worship have been erected, but never before has such a grand church been built as that which raises its dome above the city at the corner of Falmouth and Norway Streets.

Further, *The Boston Post* reported, under the headline, GATES OF BOSTON OPEN:

> The gates of Boston are open wide in welcome to nobility. Never before has the city been more frequented by members of the titled aristocracy of the old world then it is now. From all centers of Europe there are streaming into town lords and ladies who come to

attend the dedication of the new church for Christian
Scientists.

Also, people were streaming into town from all parts of the
United States and Canada. One paper estimated that nearly
forty thousand believers gathered in Boston for this momentous
occasion. No distance was too great for those who desired to do
honor to Christian Science. They came in deep appreciation of
the benefits they had received through the teachings of a saintly
woman, who had worked untiringly that they might be healed
of all error.

In the full glory of a magnificent church temple, the great
gathering of men and women from all parts of the world assembled for its dedication, to do homage to the one so dear to
them. What a temptation it would have been to any one except
Mary Baker Eddy to be present on such an occasion, to receive
the unusual and glorious honor that would have been accorded
her personal presence! But personal tribute was not God's way.
Mary Baker Eddy remained at work in the privacy of her home
in Concord.

The same respect for God's law is to be gleaned from a letter
Mrs. Eddy wrote to *The New York Herald* when making a
public reply to Mark Twain. Her letter is here quoted in part
and reference is made to the first church edifice completed and
dedicated in 1895:

> I stand in relation to this century as a Christian Dis-
> coverer, Founder, and Leader. I regard self-deification
> as blasphemous. I may be more loved, but I am less
> lauded, pampered, provided for, and cheered than
> others before me—and wherefore? Because Christian
> Science is not yet popular, and I refuse adulation.
>
> My first visit to The Mother Church after it was built
> and dedicated pleased me, and the situation was satis-
> factory. The dear members wanted to greet me with
> escort and ringing bells, but I declined and went
> alone in my carriage to the church, entered it, and
> knelt in thanks upon the steps of its altar. There the

foresplendor of the beginnings of truth fell mysteriously
upon my spirit . . .   (*Miscellany*, p. 307)

What greater reward could she aspire to than that so beautifully expressed by her in the last sentence quoted?

Again we see her thoughts in *Miscellaneous Writings*, p. 347:

God is responsible for the mission of those whom
He has anointed. Those who know no will but His
take His hand and from the night He leads to light.
None can say unto Him, What doest Thou?

There is no doubt that Mary Baker Eddy was fully aware of
her mission on earth. She was fully aware that she had been
divinely chosen to deliver Christian Science to the world. That
is why she so untiringly devoted her life to this great purpose
and why she shunned personal adulation. She had labored incessantly under great hardship to translate into human understanding the message which she knew God had given her to
deliver, and to open world-wide avenues for its acceptance.

The founder of Christian Science was not only conscientious
in safeguarding the purity of her teachings, but also in taking
steps to educate those who wished to learn Christian Science
and to know of the good work accomplished by it. To insure that
this be made possible, and that it be carried out through authentic
channels which would automatically function from year to year
as perpetual institutions, Mrs. Eddy created a Board of Education and a Board of Lectureship. These Boards are extremely
important because their work insures true presentations of the
founder's healing system and of the purpose and accomplishments of Christian Science.

In the *Church Manual*, teachers are told:

Teaching Christian Science shall not be a question
of money, but of morals and religion, healing and uplifting the race . . . He shall persistently and patiently
counsel his pupils in conformity with the unerring laws
of God, and shall enjoin them habitually to study the

Scriptures, and *Science and Health with Key to the Scriptures* as a help thereto.

In respect to the duties of lecturers, the following is quoted:

> It is the duty of the Board of Lectureship to include in each lecture a true and just reply to public topics condemning Christian Science, and to bear testimony to the facts pertaining to the life of the Pastor Emeritus.

"Healing and uplifting the race" was Mrs. Eddy's great aim in life. She worked to that end always, and never overlooked an opportunity to accomplish her purpose and to insure its perpetuation. Through many years of challenging experience, she had learned of the importance of correcting misunderstandings and condemnations of Christian Science. Such influences, if allowed to go unchallenged, were likely to grow and become damaging and thereby deprive the world of the good she had brought to it. Therefore "a true and just reply" should be given. She asked for no more and no less; she combined great strength in these two adjectives.

Men have great need of the knowledge of the great principle given to the world in the form of Christian Science. It is through the realization and utilization of the truth it reflects that he may be blessed with knowing that the Kingdom of Heaven is within him. The responsibility resting on the members of the Board of Education and of the Board of Lectureship is great beyond measure. Even greater responsibility is carried by the Christian Science Board of Directors, in whose custody Mary Baker Eddy placed the affairs of the whole Christian Science movement. Her great gift to mankind would henceforth be permanently watched over and guided by members of a Board divinely chosen for this honored service. These members are truly God's servants.

CHAPTER

21

M<small>RS. EDDY CONTINUED</small> to work in her Concord home. Each day she spent many hours at her desk, corresponding with her Directors and Trustees, guiding them in their management of the many problems arising in a rapidly growing organization. The publication of her writings and periodicals, which were growing in volume to huge proportions, received her untiring attention.

Now there was something new she was soon to be. For several years she had been waiting for the time to make an important addition to her several periodic publications. She felt there was a need for a Christian Science daily newspaper.

At this time, the following periodicals were being published regularly: *The Christian Science Quarterly*, issued quarterly, *The Christian Science Journal*, issued monthly, and *The Christian Science Sentinel*, issued weekly.

Each of these publications fulfilled a purpose, yet something more was needed to spread Christian principle to all the world. The answer was a Christian Science daily newspaper which would chronicle the news and at the same time, reflect Christian Science in all its virtues.

Mrs. Eddy decided the time now had arrived to bring into realization the dream she had cherished for so many years. She realized that it would be no easy task to do so; that there would be difficulties in the way of its consummation, calling for personal attention on her part. Frequent consultation with her publishers would be required. In order to make this possible, her presence in Boston would be necessary. Accordingly, in January, 1908, Mrs. Eddy left Concord to make her home in

Chestnut Hill, in the suburbs of Boston, where a suitable house had been purchased and furnished to her needs.

The people of Concord felt deep sorrow at the departure of their beloved citizen and benefactress. Regret equally deep filled Mary Baker Eddy's heart, for she loved this city—so close by her native Bow—and all those who had been so near to her cherished home. But, as always throughout her life, she would not allow personal desires to stand in the way of her duty.

To fill the needs of The Christian Science Publishing Society, the erection of a new publishing house had been commenced in the autumn of 1907 and the work of construction was carried out expeditiously. In August 1908, The Publishing Society moved into its handsome and commodious three-story building, which provided ample space for its future growth as well as for its present needs.

Now that the building was finished, Mary Baker Eddy lost no time in making her desires known. On August 8, she forwarded the following request to the Christian Science Board of Trustees:

> BELOVED STUDENTS:—It is my request that you start a daily newspaper at once, and call it *The Christian Science Monitor*. Let there be no delay. The Cause demands that it be issued now.
>
> You may consult with the Board of Directors, I have notified them of my intention.
>
> Lovingly yours,
Mary B. G. Eddy
(*The Life of Mary Baker Eddy*, p. 359,
by Sibyl Wilbur.)

The Board of Trustees responded enthusiastically to Mrs. Eddy's request. The Trustees consulted the Board of Directors and went to work immediately. The task progressed rapidly and harmoniously, as shown by the following concluding words of an editorial which appeared in the second number of the newly born newspaper:

To count the various items of good-will that went to build up the *Monitor* would be impossible. The architect was devoted, and his representative, the superintendent of the work, was indefatigable; the contractors were industrious in trying to meet the time limit. The builders of the press gave night and day labors. Those who had to provide materials brought in supplies, disregarding their own convenience. There was much more than buying and selling involved. There was the urgency of kindness in much of the work done. There was fine fidelity to promises given. There was honesty that rose above the claim of policy. Some might have seen confusion, but to the seeing eye, taking form among the cloud, was the vision of man serving man in a brotherhood of service. And through this demonstration of brotherhood the Leader of the Christian Science movement finds her labors for the world now assisted by the *Christian Science Monitor*.

The efficiency and harmony attending the establishment of this newspaper has continued ever since in all its affairs and operations. The spiritual love radiated by its divine founder is still reflected in all who are associated in its diverse activities.

The first issue of *The Christian Science Monitor* appeared on November 25, 1908, approximately three and one-half months after Mrs. Eddy's request to her Trustees. The accomplishment of such a tremendous undertaking in so short a time is indeed remarkable. Not only was it necessary to prepare premises, procure and install a large amount of complex physical equipment, but in addition, an expert staff had to be organized. Never before or since has history recorded any undertaking of the kind approaching this most remarkable demonstration. It can be truthfully said that Mary Baker Eddy was a great leader of men. No like work could have been accomplished without Mary Baker Eddy's inspiring leadership.

When Mary Baker Eddy made the request for a daily newspaper she also designated clearly that it was to be called *The*

Christian Science Monitor. At first there were some misgivings among a few Christian Scientists as to the suitability of the name selected, but Mrs. Eddy insisted that the one she had chosen be used, and her wishes were complied with. As always, her judgment proved to be sound, for time has demonstrated that no better name could have been adopted. The following extract from the leading editorial written by Mary Baker Eddy for the first issue of *The Christian Science Monitor*, November 25, 1908, is given here because it shows her well thought-out purpose in choosing names for her various periodicals:

> I have given the name to all the Christian Science periodicals. The first was *The Christian Science Journal*, designed to put on record the divine Science of Truth; the second I entitled *Sentinel*, intended to hold guard over Truth, Life, and Love; the third, *Der Herold der Christian Science*, to proclaim the universal activity and availability of Truth; the next I named *Monitor*, to spread undivided the Science that operates unspent. The object of the *Monitor* is to injure no man, but to bless all mankind.

With *The Christian Science Monitor*, the word of truth now reaches out daily to all countries. Men can be informed in clear, concise language about national and international affairs, knowing that the news given them is without discoloration. Truth being the guiding motive in all of this newspaper's activities, no ill feeling or ill will is engendered between peoples or between nations.

It seems to this writer that if all newspapers were patterned after the *Monitor's* example, harmony would soon reign in all national and international affairs. Understanding between men of all races, creeds, languages and nationalities would prevail. When that time arrives, well can we exclaim: "The millennium is in sight!" The even flow of this peacemaking newspaper from man-made presses is steadily augmenting in volume, as it reaches out to serve an ever-increasing number of tributaries. Through this medium, truth is delivered to all who thirst for it.

Mary Baker Eddy gave much to the world when she gave it Christian Science and the Christian Science Church, but she did not regard her mission as finished until she made it possible for the word of truth to reach all men in their daily affairs. She lovingly worked to this end and succeeded in full measure with *The Christian Science Monitor*.

CHAPTER

22

MARY BAKER EDDY arrived on earth at a time when there was a great need for spiritual enlightenment. For many centuries men had been guessing at the meaning of the Messianic mission. The science of Christian healing was no longer understood. It was true that from time to time the world had witnessed miraculous cures, but the science of these healings had not been sufficiently defined to be of broad service to mankind.

These healings were important because they served as a forceful reminder that there was such a thing as Christian healing, but in spite of these reminders, many minds took it for granted that the teachings of Jesus were part of a distant past and not applicable to modern life. The customary church orthodoxy, although founded upon the Holy Scriptures, did not encompass the perpetuation of faith healing as practiced by Jesus and later by His disciples and other early Christians.

An example (and there are many) of the missing virtue in Church orthodoxy is given by the Rev. Irving C. Tomlinson, M.A., C.S.B. in his *Twelve Years with Mary Baker Eddy*:

> After graduating from Akron University in Ohio, I took the divinity course at Tufts College, Medford, at the conclusion of which I immediately entered into the ministry of the Universalist Church. It was while pastor of the First Universalist Church of Arlington, Massachusetts, that I had an interesting experience which proved to be the direct cause of my eventually becoming a Christian Scientist. One of my parishioners was a victim of the drinking habit, and in an effort to

help him I persuaded him to undergo a popular materia
medica treatment of that day known as the Keeley
Cure. For a time at least, the man appeared to receive
some benefit and I was lauded to the skies by members
of my congregation for the splendid part I had played
in the matter. As a matter of fact, I did not think it
was "splendid" at all and the praise I received embar-
rassed me, for my own inability to heal the man seemed
most unsatisfactory to one who was supposed to be a
follower of the Master. One night during this experience I turned to my Bible for enlightenment and in the
sixteenth chapter of Mark I came across these words:
"And these signs shall follow them that believe; In my
name shall they cast out devils; they shall speak with
new tongues; they shall take up serpents; and if they
drink any deadly thing, it shall not hurt them; they shall
lay hands on the sick, and they shall recover."

I began to ponder this passage as I never had before.
Jesus' command was unmistakable, yet all I had been
able to do to help a poor victim of alcohol was to recom-
mend the Keeley Cure. I then began to wonder if there
was any church that attempted the healing work our
Master bade us perform. Next morning I began calling
on clergymen of various denominations to find the
answer to my question, but my visits proved fruitless.

The above quotation reflects in simple language man's inability to follow the commands of our Master at the time Mary
Baker Eddy was launched on her great mission. The Scriptures
were there ready for interpretation; they had awaited it for
nearly two thousand years.

For centuries men have prayed and hoped for deliverance
from their bonds and old conditions of thought. The early advances made in the physical sciences served to wean men from
reliance upon the truth which they could find in the Scriptures,
but long experience showed that their answer could only be

found through spiritual channels. Later, the physical sciences were to confirm the truth of this.

The New Testament bears witness that Jesus of Nazareth had a keen knowledge of the science of healing. He demonstrated unfailingly that this science was infallible; He healed the multitude of all manner of diseases; He possessed a perfect knowledge of God's law, and freely invoked it to relieve all who came in good faith to be healed of their suffering. He was ever conscious of His Father's presence, appealed to Him on all occasions and was deeply grateful for being heard.

> Father, I thank thee that thou has heard me. And I knew that thou hearest me always; but because of the people which stand by I said it, that they may believe that thou has sent me. (John 11: 41, 42)

Jesus was conscious that there were many who witnessed His healing work who still doubted that He had been sent by the Father. Therefore, it was necessary that he give double proof of His Sonship. The great works which benefit mankind are wrought by those who respond to divine guidance.

To recognize fully how truly the Father works through men as a means of His expression on earth, one must accept the belief that there is no other channel than that of mind by which God may express His purpose. Mary Baker Eddy repeatedly emphasized that there is but one Mind—Infinite Mind. She says:

> Infinite Mind is the creator, and creation is the infinite image or idea emanating from this Mind. If Mind is within and without all things, then all is Mind; and this definition is scientific.
>
> (*Science and Health*, pp. 256-257)

She further states:

> *God is Mind, and God is infinite; hence all is Mind.*
>
> (Ibid., p. 492)

All men are God's servants, for God is All-in-all, but some men serve Him to a greater degree than do others. Those who

serve best have left wide open those avenues which freely lead
to communion with Infinite Mind. Those who serve least or
not at all, have, through ego, closed the door on divine promptings. The value of a person's work is a measure of his Sonship
and of communion with Infinite Mind. Those who serve best
may justly feel, as the Master did when he said:

> And he that sent me is with me: the Father hath not
> left me alone; for I do always those things that please
> him. (John 8:29)

Had these very same words been uttered by Mary Baker
Eddy the world could have justly applauded, for truly she had
always done "those things that pleased Him."

In the early pages of this book, it was stated that before Mary
was born her saintly mother had a premonition that her child
was destined for great accomplishments. What these accomplishments would be was not to be disclosed until the child had
prepared herself for her mission. Beginning with her early years,
the Bible became her companion and textbook and no child became more familiar with its teachings.

Early in life Mary sensed that she had a world task to perform. When still a small child, she announced that she would
write a book when she grew up. Now that Mary Baker Eddy's
life has been unfolded and the world given her great gifts, we
can look back on those childhood days and recognize that the
incentive and qualities so necessary for the execution of her
mission were innate from early childhood. She realized at an
early age that she would have to be wise to perform her life's
work properly, and she prepared herself accordingly.

The path laid out for her was a very rough one. Yet her
varied experiences all served a useful purpose, because out of
it all was wrought the great intellect which disclosed Christian
Science.

When one looks into the sky on a clear starry night, one is
filled with awe at the wonders of the Universe. There we see
the astral bodies in their orderly array. As our vision seeks the
depth of the vastness before us, we can see no end, we can con-

ceive no end. Truly, there can be no end and no beginning in these infinite expanses. Did not Mary Baker Eddy tell us: "The infinite has no beginning"? The truth of her statement dawns on us vividly as we gaze into the sky. When we use our big telescopes to search more deeply into space, we become still more convinced that there can be no beginning, that Mrs. Eddy was right. The orderly procession of the many worlds beyond our own show no starting or terminating points in their individual journeyings. So it is for all happenings of which the mind becomes conscious. The present is sufficient unto itself. "Take therefore no thought for tomorrow; for the morrow shall take thought for the things of itself. Sufficient unto the day is the evil thereof." (Mathew 6:34)

An excellent illustration of continuity was given to the public in 1933 at the "Century of Progress" held at Chicago, when each evening at seven o'clock astronomers focused their telescope in the direction of Arcturus in the constellation of Boötes. The light and heat energy received from this faraway star had journeyed across space for forty years before entering the telescope pointed in its direction. At the small end of the telescope a photoelectric cell received the small energy that had been journeying for four decades and passed it along to vacuum tubes for amplification. In turn, the amplified energy from these vacuum tubes was sent over a Western Union telegraph wire to Chicago, where it caused an electric power switch to turn on all of the lights in the Fair grounds.

Although Arcturus was seemingly the source from which the energy was received, this energy did not have its beginning in that luminous body. For eons of time—infinite time—it had existed in some form or other and had become concentrated to produce that huge astral body from which it was radiating in all directions to travel on and on without end. Nor did the energy received at the small end of the telescope stop there; it was deflected into new channels. It could not be destroyed nor its travel arrested. Thus, in 1933, thousands of people in Chicago witnessed daily a demonstration which utilized an infinitesimal section of interval of eternity, without in any way nullifying its continuity. Mary Baker Eddy told the world this truth when she wrote *Science and Health with Key to the Scriptures*. In *Science and Health*, p. 427, she tells us:

> Man's individual being can no more die nor disappear in unconsciousness than can Soul, for both are immortal. If man believe in death now, he must disbelieve in it when learning that there is no reality in death, since the truth of being is deathless.

She also says: "Death and finiteness are unknown to Life. If Life ever had a beginning, it would also have an ending." (*Science and Health*, p. 469)

Here we are reminded of Jesus's words:

> I am the resurrection and the life: he that believeth in me, though he were dead, yet shall he live: And whosoever liveth and believeth in me shall never die. Believest thou this? (John 11:25.26)

From early childhood, the founder of Christian Science had felt the Kingdom of Heaven within her. She hungered for truth, for righteousness, for pathways which would lead her to "wonderful achievements." She searched for permanent blessings for mankind in which the struggle against error ceases, in which suffering becomes naught and vanishes into unreality, and in its place is an abounding joy and brotherly love for all men.

She held steadily to her course, never swerving from it when temptation crossed her path. Suffering, hardships and deprivations only served as agents to enlighten her in the ways of human life. She saw in these experiences the flaws of mortal mind; she saw that mortal man was his own enemy, that he had shut the door to Infinite Mind and was left in material darkness. She saw that he courted a finite world and was little conscious of his own sonship with the Father; that ego overwhelmed him. This was evident when he preferred to force his will upon his fellow men rather than to abide by the guiding influence of Divinity!

It is worthwhile to repeat her own words quoted in a previous chapter:

> Men and women of all climes and races are still in bondage to material sense, ignorant how to obtain their freedom. The rights of man were vindicated in a single section and on the lowest plane of human life, when African slavery was abolished in our land. That was only prophetic of further steps toward banishment of a worldwide slavery, found on higher planes of existence and under more subtle and depraving forms.

It was for those who were in bondage on the "high planes of existence" that this great leader devoted her life. The work she did was not only for those of her own generation but was meant to be equally helpful to those of all following generations. The law of continuity, so well entrenched in her mind, impelled her to formulate her work with a view to the present and to the future. To this end, no stones were left unturned. The freeing of the African slaves, she says, was "only prophetic of the far-reaching strides that were to follow." Through her labors—through Christian Science—she brought into the world a key which unlocked the shackles of suffering man.

In the present age, when there is strife in all civilized countries, when men war for the material commodities of life, when nations vie with one another for territorial rights and trade, when political leaders seek to be dictators, when dictators are ruthless to those they dominate, there is a pressing need for a clear understanding of the supreme governing law. There is a pressing need for an understanding that divine Mind governs all; that there is one Mind, one God; that man is God's son. It is not sufficient that these words be simply repeated without being understood, because salvation cannot be gained through superficial knowledge of the great principle. Truth must be so well learned that it becomes embodied in man's soul, as it did in God's special messenger, who disclosed it to the world so that men could be saved from the penalties of their own short vision.

In order to open the way to a true understanding of the

supremacy of divine Mind, it was necessary for Mary Baker Eddy to devote many years in close communion with her Creator until she had mentally mastered her subject.

It has been briefly mentioned in these pages how Mrs. Eddy labored to render in practical form a textbook that would be understood by those who are thoughtful and earnest and are seeking truth. There was no striving, on her part, to bring non-seekers into her fold, for she always regarded God's children as free to govern their own destinies. Christian Science would become known by the works it accomplished, and through lectures given under the auspices of the Board of Lectureship. The way is left open to all who listen and heed. All seeking enlightenment are welcomed by those who already are enlightened. The spirit of brotherly love fills their hearts.

Mary Baker Eddy was faithful to her purpose throughout every conscious moment on earth. She never procrastinated, no matter how irksome her task might be. She met each task as it arose with patience and earnestness and never laid it aside unfinished. She always lived in the *present*, knowing that if she did not avail herself of the moments given her, opportunities for *present* accomplishments would be lost forever. A conscience of duty steadfastly watched over her and, as she labored in her Father's service, gratefulness filled her heart. She was anxious that her loving followers also be awakened to the value of making good use of *present* time. Accordingly, she wrote in *The Christian Science Sentinel* of May 30, 1903:

NOW AND THEN

This was an emphatic rule of St. Paul: "Behold, now is the accepted time." A lost opportunity is the greatest of losses. Whittier mourned it as what "might have been." We own no past, no future, we possess only *now*. If the reliable *now* is carelessly lost in speaking or in acting, it comes not back again. Whatever needs to be done which cannot be done now, God prepares the way for doing; while that which can be done now, but is not, increases our indebtedness to God. Faith in

divine Love supplies the ever-present help and *now*,
and gives the power to "act in the living present."

These words speak for themselves; they tell us how their
author regarded the great gift of *now* which should not be
"carelessly lost." The lesson she gave is worthy of repetition
without end. Christian Scientists and all others will benefit by
their reiteration. Like the words of Jesus, her words were intended
not alone for the present but for the many *nows* that arise in the
future.

When restoring the sight of the blind man, Jesus said: "I
must work the works of Him that sent me, while it is day: the
night cometh, when no man can work." (John 9:4)

The works performed by Mary Baker Eddy tell how completely
she filled each *now* with the work of her Creator.

We have seen in these pages that the impelling force inherent in Mary Baker Eddy was that of love. She entered the
world with that possession and all events in her life served to
stimulate that attribute. She was surrounded by love in her
babyhood days, her childhood was favored with the love of a
pious mother, and as she advanced into her life's work, love
consistently governed her motives. Even under the severe trials
and tribulations which beset her so frequently, love was the
harmonizing agent which smoothed the path onward. God's
messenger was conscious of the presence of love within her at
all times, because she knew that God is Love. She had learned
this truth from her Bible early in life.

On page 2 of *Science and Health,* she wrote: "God is Love.
Can we ask Him to be more?" And she tells us God is Mind
and that God is All-in-all. It was the embodiment of love which
enabled Mrs. Eddy to maintain spiritual serenity and to adhere
courageously to her mission in spite of all difficulties. In everything she did she radiated the love within her. On behalf of
love she made many sacrifices.

At all times Mary Baker Eddy's soul was mantled in a gar-
ment of humility. "Whosoever therefore shall humble himself
as this little child, the same is greatest in the kingdom of

heaven." (M.18:4) Although firm in her insistence that truth prevail in all activities with which she was associated, she gave compassion and love generously. Those who came to her needing help and guidance always received her sympathetic attention.

Through Mrs. Eddy's untiring labors, the science of Mind-healing and of Christian living have been indelibly recorded in her writings. It was with deep humility that she delivered her book *Science and Health with Key to the Scriptures*. Describing its teachings, she writes in *Miscellany*, p. 115:

> I should blush to write of *Science and Health with Key to the Scriptures* as I have, were it of human origin, and were I, apart from God, its author. But, as I was only a scribe echoing the harmonies of heaven in divine metaphysics, I cannot be super-modest in my estimate of the Christian Science text book.

These are important words, because they attest in no uncertain language that Christian Science and its textbook were not of human origin, and were sent into the world through divine channels. They show that the founder of Christian Science, as God's messenger, was the scribe who echoed the truths recorded in the pages of this great textbook.

When one knows its origin, this book impels a transcending respect; a respect of all men for all time. It was written and rewritten with infinite care. Every sentence and word was weighed carefully so that the spiritual meaning would be set forth clearly. Of this care in rewriting, Daisette D. S. McKenzie, who had the privilege of knowing Mrs. Eddy, has this to say in *We Knew Mary Baker Eddy*, pp. 43-44:

> In the revision of *Science and Health*, Mrs. Eddy studied with utmost care every word of the text, and in a subsequent conversation she remarked that she often studied for months the origin and meaning of one word and its synonyms, before giving it a permanent place in the text book, and in one notable instance she

prayed and waited on God concerning a single word for three years. In thinking of this we may remind ourselves of the need for quoting her writings with correctness.

No effort could be too great to insure perfection in the language of a textbook which, with the Bible, was to serve as pastor in every Christian Science church in the world, and as pastor in the homes of hundreds of thousands of Christian Scientists.

That there must be spiritual authority for the Christian Science textbook is shown not only by the fact that the principles contained in it conform meticulously to those contained in the Holy Scriptures, but also by the beneficial results gained by thousands upon thousands of men and women through the study of its pages. In one brief paragraph in *Miscellany*, p. 111, Mrs. Eddy gives us an idea of its premise:

> The textbook of Christian Science maintains primitive Christianity, shows how to demonstrate it, and throughout is logical in premise and in conclusion. Can Scientists adhere to it, establish their practice of healing on its basis, become successful healers and models of good morals, and yet the book itself be absurd and unscientific? Is not the tree known by its fruit? Did Jesus mistake His mission and unwittingly misguide His followers? Were the apostles absurd and unscientific in adhering to His premise and proving that His conclusion was logical and divine?

The original writing and the many rewritings and clarifications of the Christian Science textbook were a tremendous task for any one person in a single lifetime. It was made even larger by the fact that so many hours of solitude and communion were necessary, even for some of its briefest passages. Yet, in spite of all these hours of labor, which spread over many years, Mrs. Eddy found time for much other work. Many were her other publications which were duly authorized and which are proving very helpful to the cause of Christian Science and the Christian Science Church.

In addition, Mrs. Eddy wrote frequently for *The Christian Science Sentinel* and for *The Christian Science Journal*. Her daily correspondence with her students, and with the officers of the several Boards and Trusteeships governing the activities of the Christian Science Church and its publishing department, equaled that of any top executive of a large industrial organization. As though that was not enough for one person, Mrs. Eddy watched the daily papers and personally replied to incorrect statements regarding Christian Science or her own life.

Because she was determined that Christian Science stand out in its true light against all destructive influences, it was important to answer the endless attacks upon her theology and her motives. It was essential that when the time arrived for her to journey on from this mortal world, the message she had brought be left on unshakeable, permanent foundations. That is why this valiant leader rallied to the defense of God's message whenever it was attacked. She remembered well how Christ Jesus was assailed because of His loving mission, as well as the repeated cruelties imposed upon the early Christians. She knew that her theology, which offered truth to the multitudes, would not be accepted without dissensions; that it would have to pass through much turmoil before its truth could be recognized by all.

Mrs. Eddy met the many storms which crossed her path with firmness, patience and understanding, and the clouds were cleared away without rancor on her part. She accepted each challenge as a God-given opportunity to clarify her theology, and to prove that Christian Science unfolded the truths contained in the Holy Scriptures. She was always ready to forgive her assailants, for she knew they were badly misguided. Early in life she learned this virtue, which made forgiveness natural to her. In recording her understanding of the Lord's Prayer, her interpretation of "And forgive us our debts, as we forgive our debtors" is given as: "And Love is reflected in love."

This is a beautiful and spiritual interpretation. It truly reflects the meaning of forgiveness—for there can be no forgiveness without love. Christian Science was evolved through love, the love of its founder, a love which came from God. Her generous and courageous heart never withheld forgiveness. Of the many things we owe our fellow human beings, she realized that forgiveness stands high on the list. Also, she believed that in the Apostles' Creed we acknowledge belief in "the forgiveness of sins."

Laurence Sterne once said:

> The brave only, know how to forgive; it is the most refined and generous pitch of virtue human nature can arrive at. Cowards have done good and kind actions, cowards have even fought, nay sometimes even conquered; but a coward never forgave. It is not in his nature; the power of doing it flows only from strength and greatness of soul, conscious of its own force and security and above the little temptations of resenting every fruitless attempt to interrupt its happiness.

Mary Baker Eddy's whole life reflected her love for her fellow man. From early childhood she had prepared herself for her mission of relieving men and women of the many ills besetting them. We have seen in these pages how she unceasingly labored to achieve that goal, and how she ultimately succeeded in doing so. Through constant communion with God, a science was revealed to her. She named it Christian Science because it had as its root the Science used by Christ Jesus. To reach the multitude with this new revelation of truth, which had been practiced nearly two thousand years before, Mrs. Eddy wrote *Science and Health with Key to the Scriptures*. Without the aid of this book, the new Science would have been restricted to a few persons of her generation. Her inward urge to aid all who might seek the benefits of her theology was divinely fulfilled through the medium of her textbook. In this way Mary Baker Eddy found a practical outlet for that which was closest to her heart—an inborn love for her fellow man.

It is fortunate indeed that we have her own words on the subject. *The Evening Press*, of Grand Rapids, Michigan, asked her in August 1907: "What is nearest and dearest to your heart today?" Here is Mrs. Eddy's reply in part:

Editor of the *Evening Press*:

To your courtesy and to your question permit me to say that, insomuch as I know myself, what is "Nearest and dearest" to my heart is an honest man or woman —one who steadfastly and actively strives for perfection, one who leavens the loaf of life with justice, mercy, truth and love. (*Miscellany*, pp. 271-272)

All true Christian Scientists are nearest and dearest to Mrs. Eddy, because they are honest and strive for perfection. Her reward is great, indeed, for today there are hundreds of thousands of men and women who, because of her teachings, embody the qualities she named as being those closest to her heart. And there will be millions in future generations who will become better individuals and citizens because Mrs. Eddy had come on earth.

Christian Scientists are recognized as peace-loving and upright citizens the world over. As a class and as individuals, they radiate good wherever they are. They "strive for self abnegation, justice, meekness, mercy, purity, love." (*Miscellaneous Writings*, p. 154)

They hold the respect of all who know them, and are doing much toward bringing peace among men on earth. They are truly God's unselfish children, for they live in an atmosphere of harmony, showing kindly thoughts, words and deeds. Love is their creative principle. When assailed, they do not retaliate, but instead do good in return. They do not pass judgment on others and condemn no one. They curb anger, fear and jealously and know they are one with God. In every way they reflect the theology of their leader. What greater reward could be given her?

CHAPTER

23

A ND GOD SAID, Let there be light; and there was light. "And
God saw the light, that it was good: and God divided
the light from the darkness." (Genesis 1:3-4)

Twenty centuries ago God sent into the world a lightbearer
in the person of Christ Jesus. Man's understanding of God's
laws had become dimmed through theological rituals which
were preached without regard to their spiritual meaning. Men
were living in selfish materialism, gratifying their desires and
senses at the expense of their fellow beings. Self-preservation
was dominant in nearly all individuals because they discerned
not the great truth, that they were one with God.

Money, food, clothing, shelter, security, pleasure, were the
goals in life. Religion was a means to this end, employed as
one would employ machinery for the production of chattels.
Priests who were supposedly learned in the Scriptures did not
know their true meaning. Synagogues were lavishly appointed,
and an outward exhibition of piety was freely made, which with
exception, was artificial and not heartfelt. The way to Heaven
was on sale and many who paid their tithes felt that this was all
that was required of them, that beyond this they were free
to pursue their pleasures as they saw fit.

These people were slaves of selfishness. Both the lowly and
the high toiled for self-preservation of aggrandizement, and because of their own shallow lives they were groping in spiritual
darkness.

No wonder a leader had been sent among them, one who
would preach God's law as it had never been understood in
their generation, the Messiah who had been promised and long

looked for. But their vision had been so dimmed that they did not recognize Him in their midst. Although He was a man Who had been chosen to bring light out of darkness, although He repeatedly demonstrated His power over human weakness, still they could not believe He was the one looked for. How could one of lowly birth, a carpenter until He was thirty years of age, be vested with the power of the expected deliverer of the Hebrews? It was difficult indeed to understand how God could work through a man who had come on earth as a human being.

During His ministry, it was not generally known that when He was twelve years of age, at the feast of the Passover, He had been found in the Temple "sitting in the midst of doctors, both hearing them and asking questions. And all who heard Him were astonished at His understanding and answers." But even had this intercourse been publicly known at the time of His ministry, it is doubtful that it would have been given due weight.

He taught the people that their bodies were temples of the living God, and that He was one with His Heavenly Father, and demonstrated that He had been given power over sin, sickness and death. His works were regarded as miracles and many sufferers sought Him to be healed and marveled at their recovery. But the world was not yet ready to believe that He was the Messiah prophesied in the Scriptures. Darkness so overshadowed the understanding of the people that they even failed to comprehend the import of the words of John the Baptist when he appeared at the River Jordan and announced the coming of Christ, and they recognized not the Prophet when He arrived in their midst. During His ministry, spiritual light shone on the world through the works He performed. These were recorded and henceforth the world was made a better place in which to live.

With the advancing years the light of Christianity spread over more and more of God's children. However, as time passed, men professing to be Christians disagreed as to church tenets, and divisions were made, each group using Christianity as a base but having variations in dogma. Again ritual became more important than the disclosure of God's laws, and, in consequence, the teachings of Christ Jesus were dimmed to the multitude.

With the advent of the nineteenth century, the foregoing conditions prevailed. The confusion already brought about by rivalries between Christian dogmas was added to by the advances made in the physical sciences. These advances were causing many to believe that man's reasoning, aided by modern knowledge, might reveal the light of man's being. They began to think that possibly the light sought in the Scriptures, while suited to those of past generations, did not so well reveal the truth to those who could benefit from the knowledge afforded through the modern sciences. "Beware lest any man spoil you through philosophy and vain deceit, after tradition of men, after the rudiments of the world, and not after Christ." (Colossians 2:8) On this Lord Bacon said: "A little Philosophy inclineth a man's mind to atheism, but depth in philosophy bringeth men's minds about to religion." To this confusion, more was being added by a growing interest in spiritualism, mesmerism, animal magnetism and hypnotism. In cities and in rural areas alike, these subjects were attracting the attention of many people and were often regarded seriously.

Men no longer knew how to overcome the ills of their transgressions or omissions; they did not know that there was an imperishable principle knocking at their door. They did not understand that the confusion with which they had surrounded themselves drew a veil over the truth they wished revealed to them; they did not know that the righteousness they hoped to find was fixed, unvarying, and ever present, awaiting only their recognition.

They did not realize that they needed to free themselves of the evil passions which hold men in bondage. They overlooked the fact that their bodies were God's temples and therefore should not be desecrated. As a people, they were confused and could not see clearly the light contained in the Holy Scriptures. They were sacrificing themselves for meaningless material things, which they accepted in lieu of spiritual verities. Little time was available for meditation and communion with God.

Thus, mankind was in a sorry plight when Mary Baker Eddy came upon earth. The haze was thick and obscured the light of truth, and vision was circumscribed within the narrow boundaries of material senses. Certainly there was great need to separate light from darkness; to bring into the open that which had been lost, the teachings of His Son, Christ Jesus.

As we look over history we can note many parallels between the life of Jesus and that of Mary Baker Eddy. Here are several of them:

"An angel said unto Mary: 'And, behold thou shalt conceive in thy womb, and bring forth a son, and shall call his name Jesus. He shall be great, and shall be called the son of the Highest.'" Abigail Baker also had a premonition that the child in her womb was consecrated and destined for "wonderful achievements."

At twelve years of age, Jesus was about His Father's business and sat in the Temple in the midst of doctors, "both hearing them and asking questions." At the same age Mary was about her Father's business and sat in the Presbyterian Church in Bow, answering her pastor's questions and making known her understanding of God's love for His children.

Jesus was well versed in the Scriptures; so was Mary. Jesus taught the allness of spirit and the nothingness of matter; so did Mary. Jesus resorted to solitude when seeking communion with God; so did Mary. Jesus demonstrated His oneness with God by healing the sick; so did Mary. Jesus claimed that the works He performed were not of Him but of the Father; Mary emphasized the same truth. Jesus was aided by His disciples, Mary by her students. Jesus's mission was resisted; so was Mary's.

The truths taught by Jesus have traveled through the centuries and will continue ever onward; the truths taught by Mary also are traveling onward. Each had a mission suited to the times; each fulfilled it without faltering and gave the world light where there was darkness. In Jesus was seen the Biblical prophecy of the first coming of Christ on Earth; in Mary was seen the Biblical prophecy of the second coming of Christ on Earth, through her delivery of Christian Science.

When Mary Baker Eddy had fulfilled her mission, when she knew her work was well done and that it would endure through the centuries ahead, she was ready to journey on. Her whole life had been devoted to God's service, for the benefit of His children, and she said repeatedly: "God is All-in-all." She based her life on this high principle.

Two days before journeying to the world beyond, she called for a pad and wrote on it: "God is my life." She was thorough in all her life's work. This last writing was for the record, so that there would be no misunderstanding. She lived in God and God in her. She was God's messenger of love.

"The grass withereth, the flower fadeth; but the word of our God shall stand forever." (Isaiah 40:8)

And the word of our God, revealed through Mary Baker Eddy, shall stand forever!

ACKNOWLEDGMENTS

The author wishes to acknowledge his grateful appreciation for the consent given him to employ quotations from the following:

THE GLORIES OF MARY, by Alphonsus de Liguori (Very Rev. Andrew B. Kuhn, C.SS.R., 1931).

MRS. EDDY, by Hugh A. Studdert Kennedy (Farallon Press, 1910, 1947).

THE LIFE OF MARY BAKER EDDY, by Sibyl Wilbur (Christian Science Publishing Society, 1907 through 1941).

THE LIFE OF LUTHER, by Barnes Sears (Philadelphia, 1850).